# The Everyday Halogen Oven Cookbook

# The Everyday Halogen Oven Cookbook

Quick, easy and nutritious recipes for all the family

## SARAH FLOWER

A How To Book

ROBINSON

ROBINSON

First published in Great Britain in 2010 by Spring Hill, an imprint of How To Books Ltd

This edition published in 2013 by Robinson

Copyright © Sarah Flower 2010

7 9 10 8

The moral right of the author has been asserted.

A CIP catalogue record for this book
is available from the British Library.

ISBN: 978-1-90586-247-4

Produced for How To Books by Deer Park Productions, Tavistock, Devon
Designed and Typeset by Mousemat Design Ltd
Printed and bound in Great Britain by Ashford Colour Press Ltd, Gosport, Hants

Robinson
An imprint of
Little, Brown Book Group
Carmelite House
50 Victoria Embankment
London EC4Y 0DZ

An Hachette UK Company
www.hachette.co.uk

www.littlebrown.co.uk

NOTE: The material contained in this book is set out in good faith for general guidance and no liability can be accepted for loss or expense incurred as a result of relying in particular circumstances on statements made in the book. Laws and regulations are complex and liable to change, and readers should check the current position with relevant authorities before making personal arrangements.

How To Books are published by Robinson, an imprint of Little, Brown Book Group. We welcome proposals from authors who have first-hand experience of their subjects. Please set out the aims of your book, its target market and its suggested contents in an email to howtobooks@littlebrown.co.uk

Thanks to my Mum for teaching me the joys of cooking
as a child and for helping me plan new recipes for this book.

# Contents

# Introduction

As a journalist, I am fortunate enough to hear about new products and to have the chance to review them. I had seen press releases about a new oven that was supposed to save time and money, so I was pleased when a halogen oven was sent to me from JML. My first thought was one of confusion – how on earth did this strange looking thing work and, surely, being round, it was limiting to use? How wrong I was.

Since then I have spread the virtues of the halogen oven to anyone who cares to listen. I have never been a fan of microwaves, but the halogen oven is a completely different entity. It cooks some things up to 40% quicker and others pretty much the same as a conventional oven. It reheats, grills, bakes, roasts, steams, defrosts and slow cooks – it even makes toast and hard-boiled eggs. In short, it is a great machine for families as well as single people or couples, students and even holiday homes.

For me and my family, the halogen has not replaced my conventional oven but it has limited its use dramatically. When I am having a baking day, I use the conventional oven, making sure I fill it up to warrant turning it on. However most days see some form of use with the halogen, whether it's a quick snack or an evening meal. It is also incredibly useful over the Christmas period and when we have a dinner party.

If you are new to the halogen, don't be scared of it. Treat it like a very efficient conventional oven and experiment with the timings. The glass bowl gives you a bird's eye view of what is happening inside, allowing you to act quickly to avoid a disaster if and where necessary.

The recipes in this book should give you a wide variety of ideas that you can adapt to suit your own preferences.

I have noticed that some halogen oven recipes on the internet recommend high temperatures, reducing the overall time in the oven. However, I have kept to a more conventional approach having found that high temperatures can often lead to burnt tops and raw middles. The obsession of speed rather than quality of the finished product is probably due to people treating the halogen like a microwave. I prefer to reduce the temperatures so that they are similar to the approach used with conventional ovens. This enables you to create many dishes, including cakes, without a problem, while capitalising on the fact that by being small and compact the halogen uses less energy than a conventional oven, even though the timings aren't any different.

This book contains numerous recipes and tips which will help you enjoy the many benefits of the halogen oven. The recipes have come from years of cooking, as well as from friends, family, adaption and experimentation. I adore baking cakes so this was one area I really wanted to prove the halogen could cope with. I soon realised that family favourites can work well in the halogen with only very minor tweaking where necessary. The more you use it, the more confident you will become.

I hope you enjoy this book and I wish you many great meals ahead.

# Using Your Halogen Oven

You have probably received your halogen oven with the minimum of advice on how to use this bench-top machine. If you are lucky you may have a booklet containing a couple of recipes. I hope this chapter helps make life with your halogen simple and clear.

## Choosing the right machine for you

There are many different halogen ovens on the market, but they are basically all the same machine. The two main variations are the size of bowl and whether the lid is on a hinge. My first machine was from JML when they first started to become popular. I was not really sure what to expect and, over time, it has gained more and more use in our home. Personally, I would opt for the largest bowl as this increases the oven's usability. You can also purchase extenders, which can help maximise use. Extenders are metal rings that fit over the top of the halogen bowl, literally extending the height of the bowl and enabling you to fit more into your oven. The lid then fits on top of the extender. They are also useful if you want to keep the food away from the heating element to prevent burning.

After using the JML oven, I progressed to the Flavorwave Turbo Platinum Oven. Some of the advantages that this particular oven has over others are that it has the hinged lid, digital settings, a 3-speed fan and a pre-heat setting.

Looking at online forums I have noticed that the lids do cause a bit of a bug bear. I had a lid stand beside my JML machine, though annoyingly these are optional extras that you have to purchase and are quite flimsy to look at. Personally, I think it is better to buy the halogen cooker with the hinged lid if you can afford it – this is definitely a safer and easier option.

### How do they work?

The halogen oven is basically a large glass bowl with an electric halogen lid. The lid is heavy as it contains the halogen element, timer and temperature settings. The halogen element heats up the bowl and the fan moves the air around the bowl to create an even temperature. As it is smaller than a conventional oven it heats up faster, reducing the need for long preheating and in some cases reducing the overall cooking time.

This makes it a very popular choice for those watching their pennies, living on their own or, like me, cooking for a busy family. It has even become a popular choice for students and caravanners. I read on a forum that some caravanners use the self-clean facility just like a mini dishwasher – ingenious! It is also popular as a second oven and really becomes invaluable at busy times like Christmas or dinner parties.

For safety, the lid's handle has to be in place (placed securely down) for the machine to turn on. This means that when you lift the lid, the oven is automatically turned off. If you are using the Flavorwave machine with the hinged lid, you have to press the start button to start it and remember to turn the machine off when you lift the lid.

The halogen oven does cook slightly differently to a conventional oven, so first beginning to use it often involves a process of trial and error, but it is not vastly different. If you have favourite recipes that you cook in the conventional oven, try them in the halogen. I find cooking at a slightly lower temperature or cooking for less time normally gives the same results, but hopefully this book will help give you more confidence.

The halogen oven is not a microwave and does not work in the same way as a microwave, so if you are thinking you can cook food in a few minutes you are wrong. It does however have a multitude of functions – defrosting, baking, grilling, roasting and steaming are all perfect for the halogen. Remember that to get the optimum benefit air needs to circulate around the bowl, so ideally place dishes and trays on racks and avoid the temptation to over fill.

## Getting the right equipment

This sounds obvious but ... make sure you have oven trays, baking sheets and casserole dishes that will fit inside the halogen oven. There is nothing more frustrating than planning a meal and just at the last minute realising that your dish does not fit in the machine! You can use any ovenproof dish or tray – metal, silicon and Pyrex are all fine. The halogen oven is round so it makes sense to look at trays and stands of the same shape, but smaller so you can remove them without burning yourself.

When I first started using the halogen, it was frustrating to find that 80% of my bakeware did not fit in the machine. A quick revamp and purchase of the accessories have proved invaluable. If money is tight, you can find great casserole dishes at boot sales or charity shops – you don't have to spend a fortune on new cookware.

You can also buy the accessories pack which contains steamer pans, browning trays, grilling pans, toasting racks and even an extension ring. These are highly recommended if you use your oven regularly and certainly enhance what you can do with the machine. There are many websites selling or advertising these accessories, so a general internet search will point you in the right direction. Amazon is also a great place to look.

### Let there be light

As experienced halogen users will know, the halogen light turns on and off during cooking. This is not a fault of the thermostat as some people have mentioned on forums. It literally turns off when the programmed temperature is reached, then on again when it drops. Set the temperature and marvel at how quickly the oven reaches the required temperature – literally in minutes. I love the light; there is something quite cosy about walking into your kitchen on a winter or autumn evening and seeing the glow of the halogen cooker alongside watching your food cook.

### Timings

The halogen oven comes with a timer (60 minute) and temperature setting dials. The Flavorwave Turbo also comes with three fan settings and a digital timer. All halogens turn off when the timer settings have been reached. This means you can be reassured that if the phone rings or you are called away from the kitchen, your food won't spoil.

### Size

The oven is small enough to sit on a worktop, but do allow space for removal of the lid if it is not hinged. The lid can get very hot and is quite large and heavy, being the brains of the machine, so it can be a good idea to buy the lid stand. However be careful when using this stand as it can seem quite flimsy until you get used to it. You could opt to place the lid on a heatproof surface but, again, be careful not to burn yourself or your worktop!

### Careful does it

Your oven should come with some tong type of gadget to help you lift out the racks. They are quite useful, but I also use a more substantial set of tongs. As with any oven or cooker, do be careful as the bowl and contents gets very hot. I find using proper oven gloves a necessity as they cover your whole hand and wrist and can prevent accidents.

As with all electrical and hot appliances, do not let your children near the halogen – the glass bowl gets very hot.

### Defrosting

Most halogen ovens have a defrost facility, which is very useful. Refer to your manufacturer's details. Many people seem to want recommended timings for defrosting but it really depends on what you are defrosting and how big it is. I would advise setting the defrost button to 5 or 10 minute intervals and testing as you go.

I don't tend to buy frozen ready meals but judging by comments on forums, this is a popular choice for halogen owners. When cooking frozen ready meals, the thing to remember is that the nearer the food is to the element, the browner it will get – and the higher the temperature, the quicker it could burn! Don't panic, one of the joys of a halogen oven is the ability to see the food clearly through the glass bowl so, if in doubt, watch the food to prevent it from burning. See Chapter 2 on snacks for more information and advice.

### Foil and coverings

Some people like to use foil when cooking. This can be a good idea as it prevents food from browning too quickly or can be used to parcel foods, but make sure the foil is secure. The fan is very strong and if the foil is not secure it could float around the oven and might damage the element. Another option for preventing burning is obviously to turn the temperature down or place the food further away from the element (use the low rack or add an extension ring).

### Cleaning your oven

The halogen is promoted as being self-cleaning. This basically means that you fill it with a little water, a squirt of washing-up liquid and turn on to the wash setting. The combination of the fan and the heat allows the water to swish around the bowl giving it a quick clean. This normally takes about 10 minutes. Personally, I find it just as simple to remove the bowl and place in the dishwasher – it always comes out gleaming.

The lid is a little more difficult to clean and I would refer to the manufacturer's guidelines as each product can be a little different. Do not get the element or electrical parts wet!

### How to cook

Individual chapters in this book provide details about how to cook different types of food in your halogen. You can follow the recipes or see if you can create your own recipes using those provided for guidance.

If you are concerned about cooking meat, I would advise using a meat thermometer. If the temperature is too high, the meat or joint will brown quickly on the surface but may not be cooked in the middle. Don't panic too much – you will soon get used to it.

### High and low racks

There are two standard racks which come with every halogen oven – a high and a low rack. The high rack is placed nearer the element so use this if you want to brown something. The low rack is used more for longer cooking times.

You can also cook directly on the bottom of the bowl. I do this quite often, particularly if I am being lazy and just want to chuck in some oven chips. It does cook well but takes a little longer as compared to using the racks, as air is not able to circulate all around the food.

### Baking

Some people worry about using the halogen to bake cakes but I think this is because they are setting the oven temperature too high, resulting in a crusty brown cake top with a soggy middle. Setting the oven to a lower temperature can solve this problem. Muffins and cupcakes take between 12 and 18 minutes. You only really encounter problems with cakes if you are cooking for too long at too high a temperature. Try some of my cake recipes and you will see how simple it can be.

## Preheat or not to preheat

Most recipes I have found on forums don't mention preheating the oven. This is probably due to the speed the oven takes to reach its temperature setting. However, I think it is worth turning the oven on 5 minutes before use just to bring it up to the right temperature.

I found this to be the case when attempting to cook soft-boiled eggs. According to the Flavorwave recipe book, I should be able to cook a soft egg in 6 minutes just by placing it on the high rack. It didn't work, but when I tried again in a heated oven it was much more successful.

Some machines (such as the Flavorwave) have a preheat button which preheats at 260°C for 6 minutes, but others, such as the JML, require you to set to the required temperature and turn on.

## Weights, and Measures

I am constantly being asked for the recipes for my cakes and it always throws me into turmoil as I never measure anything when baking. My husband laughs as he sees me literally throwing in all sorts of ingredients, seemingly oblivious to the end result. Thankfully they all come out perfectly yummy!

Don't follow my lead – until you are confident, measure as you go. There is some great measuring equipment available to make life easier.

### Measuring spoons

You can buy a neat little set of measuring spoons for around £2. They are ideal for recipes that need teaspoon, tablespoon or dessertspoon measurements.

### Measuring cups

These are good for measuring dry ingredients or liquids. Some show measures for key ingredients such as flour or sugar, others just measure in millilitres.

### Measuring jug

I use a glass Pyrex measuring jug. They are very hardy and come up gleaming after every wash – unlike plastic jugs which can stain. Measuring jugs are ideal for measuring liquids or mixing ingredients together. I also have a great Pyrex measuring jug which shows grams for sugar, flour and mixed fruit. I have picked up various pieces of kitchenalia from boot sales and auctions over the years.

### Scales

Find a set of scales that suits your kitchen. I like the retro-looking scales with a deep bowl which is ideal for weighing a variety of ingredients. Scales can cost as little as £3 to buy new.

### Weights table

1 ounce is equal to approximately 28g, but for ease of use, most tables round down to 25g per ounce and gradually increase this as the weight increases. See the table below for clarity.

| WEIGHT | |
| --- | --- |
| Metric (approx.) | Imperial |
| 25–30g | 1oz |
| 50–55g | 2oz |
| 85g | 3oz |
| 100g | 3.5oz |
| 125g | 4oz |
| 150g | 5oz |
| 175g | 6oz |
| 200g | 7oz |
| 225g | 8oz |
| 250g | 9oz |
| 280g | 10oz |
| 350g | 12oz |
| 400g | 14oz |
| 450g | 16oz/1lb |
| 900kg | 2lb |

| LIQUID MEASURE | |
| --- | --- |
| Metric (approx.) | Imperial |
| 5ml | 1 teaspoon (tsp) |
| 15ml | 1 tablespoon (tbsp) |
| 25–30ml | 1 fl oz |
| 50ml | 2 fl oz |
| 75ml | 3 fl oz |
| 100–125ml | 4 fl oz |
| 150ml | 5 fl oz |
| 175ml | 6 fl oz |
| 200ml | 7 fl oz |
| 225ml | 8 fl oz |
| 250ml | 9 fl oz |
| 300ml | 10 fl oz (½ pint) |
| 600ml | 20 fl oz (1 pint) |
| 1 litre | 1¾ pints |

I hope this chapter has not confused you. Move on to try some recipes and then come back to this chapter at a later date – it will probably make more sense then!

Enjoy!

# Snacks

Although we aim to be healthy, there are times when a quick and easy snack really hits the mark. Unlike microwaves, halogen ovens can heat up pastries, pizzas and snacks without resulting in a soggy mess. They can also make delicious toasties with ease. Here are some suggestions to inspire you.

# Toast

This is really where the accessories for halogen ovens come into their own. If you purchase an accessory pack, you can get a breakfast rack. This looks like a toast rack with some compartments for your eggs. If you don't have this accessory, you could opt for an ovenproof toast rack – make sure there is at least a 2cm gap from the halogen lid. You may have to cut your slices in half to accommodate them.

- Simply put your slices of bread on the high rack.
- Cook at 250°C for about 4–6 minutes until the toast reaches the desired colour. The toast should brown on both sides without you needing to turn it.

This is trial and error. When I first tried it, some of the slices were toasted but not golden – they tasted the same but the odd slice lacked colour. I adjusted the temperature setting and then things improved.

# Cheese on Toast

Because the halogen oven has a powerful fan setting, you don't have to toast one side of the bread before adding your topping. You can have delicious toasted cheese in 5 minutes.

- Cut the bread into slices and cover with grated cheese or your chosen topping. Season to taste.
- Place on the high rack, topping facing upwards.
- Cook at 250°C for 5–7 minutes until the topping is bubbling.

# Toasted Sandwich

- Place one slice with your chosen topping and one slice without the topping side by side on the high rack.
- Cook at 250°C for 4–5 minutes until the topping is bubbling.
- Place the plain bread slice over the topped slice to form a sandwich and cook for a further 1–2 minutes if necessary.

# Welsh Rarebit

- Preheat the halogen oven using the preheat setting or set the temperature to 250°C.
- Place the slices of bread on the high rack or toast rack for 3–4 minutes to toast.
- Meanwhile, in a saucepan on your hob add the milk, butter, cheese and mustard and stir until dissolved and thick. Be careful not to have this too high or it will stick and burn.
- Spoon the cheese mixture onto one side of the toast and season to taste. Place back on the high rack and cook for another 3 minutes or until golden and bubbling.
- Serve with a side salad and some delicious chutney.

2–4 slices of bread
3–4 tablespoons milk
10g butter
250g mature cheese
1 teaspoon mustard

# Egg and Cheese Rarebit

2–4 slices of bread
2–3 eggs
3–4 tablespoons milk
10g butter
250g mature cheese
1 teaspoon mustard

- Preheat the halogen oven using the preheat setting or set the temperature to 180°C.
- Place the eggs in the egg rack or on the high rack and cook for 7–8 minutes until they are soft or medium. (The egg rack comes with the accessory pack. It is specially designed and is higher than the low rack.)
- Meanwhile, in a saucepan on your hob add the milk, butter, cheese and mustard and stir until dissolved and thick. Be careful not to have this too high or it will stick and burn. Leave to one side with a lid on to keep warm.
- Remove the eggs and turn up the temperature to 250°C. Place the slices of bread on the high rack and cook for 3–4 minutes to toast.
- Remove the shells of the eggs and roughly slice them directly on to the toast, especially if the egg yolk is still soft.
- Spoon the cheese mixture onto the egg slices and season to taste. Place back on the high rack and cook for 3–4 minutes until golden and bubbling.
- Serve with a side salad and some delicious chutney.

# Mozzarella, Tomato and Basil Toastie

This is one of my favourite quick snacks. You can leave it open or covered to make a toasted sandwich – the choice is yours! If I don't have any fresh basil leaves, I add some baby leaf spinach.

- Preheat the halogen oven using the preheat setting or set the temperature to 250°C.
- Create your toastie by placing tomatoes on buttered or unbuttered bread (depending on preference). Add some basil or spinach leaves and cover with mozzarella. Season to taste.
- Place on the high rack and cook for 3–4 minutes until golden and bubbling.
- Drizzle with a little olive oil. Serve with a side salad.

*Note:* For extra zing, why not spread a little pesto onto the bread before adding the tomatoes, leaves and mozzarella.

2–4 slices of wholemeal or granary bread
1–3 tomatoes (depending on size and portion numbers), sliced
Basil leaves (or spinach leaves)
1 ball of mozzarella, sliced or torn
Seasoning to taste
Olive oil
Pesto (optional)

# Sardines in Tomato Sauce on Toast

2–4 slices of
  wholemeal or
  granary bread
120g sardines in
  tomato sauce
Spring onions, finely
  chopped (optional)
Sundried tomatoes
  (optional)

- Preheat the halogen oven using the preheat setting or set the temperature to 250°C.
- Remove the sardines from the tin and mash slightly. (You can add some finely chopped spring onions and a dollop of sundried tomatoes if you prefer). Place the sardines on the bread slices.
- Place on the high rack and cook for 3–4 minutes until golden and bubbling.
- Serve with a side salad.

# Bacon

Who can resist a bacon butty? You can cook bacon without adding more fat in approximately 6 minutes using the halogen oven.

- Place the bacon on the high rack.
- Set the temperature to 240°C.
- Cook for 5 minutes, then turn over and cook for another 5 minutes or until your desired crispiness is reached.

# Soft or Hard-boiled Eggs

You would not really think the halogen oven could be used to boil an egg, but you will be surprised. You can place the eggs directly onto the rack, or you could opt for the breakfast rack as an optional accessory.

- Preheat the halogen oven using the preheat setting or set the temperature to 180°C.
- Place the eggs on the high rack or breakfast rack.
- Cook for 6 minutes to achieve a soft-boiled egg or 10 minutes for a hard-boiled egg. Take care when removing them from the oven as they will be very hot.

*Note:* This did not work when I first tried it. I discovered that you really do have to preheat the oven and it is best if the eggs are at room temperature before cooking. If they have been in a cold fridge, you may have to cook them for a minute or two more – you will soon discover the timing that suits your taste.

# Bruschetta

I love the simplicity of bruschetta – it really is just something on toast but it tastes so much nicer! I use a French stick, ciabatta or doorstop slices of homemade bread. Experiment with your own toppings. This recipe is my favourite cheat for a quick snack.

- Preheat the halogen oven using the preheat setting or set the temperature to 240–250°C.
- Spread red pesto thinly over the bread slices. Add the spring onions and mozzarella.
- Finish with a few cherry tomato quarters on each slice. Season to taste and drizzle with a little good quality olive oil.
- Place on the high rack and cook for 4–6 minutes until golden.
- Serve immediately.

4–6 thick slices of bread
Red pesto
3–4 spring onions, sliced
1 ball of mozzarella, torn
6–10 cherry tomatoes, quartered
Seasoning to taste
Drizzle of olive oil

# Garlic Mushroom and Mozzarella Bruschetta

10g butter
2–3 cloves of garlic, crushed
6–8 mushrooms
4–6 slices of bread
Handful of basil or spinach leaves, shredded
1 ball of mozzarella, torn
Seasoning to taste

- Preheat the halogen oven using the preheat setting or set the temperature to 240–250°C.
- Melt the butter and add the garlic – you can use the halogen to do this but don't let the butter burn.
- Place the mushrooms on a baking tray and brush with the melted garlic butter.
- Place the tray on the high rack and cook for 5 minutes to help soften the mushrooms.
- On the bread slices, place the shredded leaves followed by the garlic mushrooms. Finish with some torn mozzarella. Season to taste.
- Place back on the high rack and cook for 5 minutes or until melted and cooked.

# Mozzarella, Basil and Tomato Panini

Create your own café favourite snack in your halogen.

- Preheat the halogen oven using the preheat setting or set the temperature to 250°C.
- Slice open the panini rolls and fill with mozzarella, basil leaves and sliced tomatoes. Season to taste.
- Place the filled rolls on the high rack and cook for 4–6 minutes until golden and the mozzarella has started to melt. You may want to turn them halfway through.
- Serve with a side salad and tortilla chips.

2–4 panini rolls
1 ball of mozzarella, torn
Handful of basil leaves
2–3 tomatoes, sliced
Seasoning to taste

# Cheese and Ham Panini

2–4 panini rolls
Mature cheddar, sliced
  or grated
4–6 slices of ham
Seasoning to taste

- Preheat the halogen oven using the preheat setting or set the temperature to 250°C.
- Slice open the panini rolls and fill with the cheese and slices of ham. Season to taste.
- Place the filled rolls on the high rack and cook for 4–6 minutes until golden and the cheese has started to melt. You may want to turn them halfway through.
- Serve with a side salad and tortilla chips.

# Fresh Garlic Bread

You can make your own garlic bread from French bread by following this basic recipe.

French stick
1 tablespoon butter
2–3 cloves of garlic, crushed
1–2 teaspoons mixed herbs

- Partially slice the French stick into 2–3cm thick slices, making sure you don't cut right through the bread.
- Mix 1 tablespoon of butter with 1 or 2 crushed garlic cloves and a sprinkle of mixed herbs.
- Thickly spread the butter in between the slices of bread.
- Place on a baking tray, making sure it fits into your halogen oven. Place the tray on the lower rack and turn the oven on to 230°C.
- Cook for 5–8 minutes until golden.
- To serve, simply allow the diners to tear off the bread slices.

*Variation:* Try spreading with either green or red pesto instead of garlic butter.

# Frozen Garlic Bread

- Place the frozen garlic bread on a baking tray, making sure it fits into your halogen oven.
- Place the tray on the lower rack and turn the oven on to 230°C.
- Cook for 8–12 minutes until golden.
- To serve, simply allow the diners to tear off the bread slices.

# Warming Naan Bread

Naan bread is delicious with curries and Indian meals and you can now buy it ready made. The halogen oven is a great tool for warming naan bread.

- Sprinkle the naan bread with a little cold water.
- Place on the high rack and cook for 5–8 minutes at 230°C. You may want to turn these halfway through cooking.
- Serve immediately.

# Frozen Pizza

Refer to your manufacturer's cooking instructions for more information.

- Preheat the halogen oven using the preheat setting or set the temperature to 200°C for 5 minutes while you prepare your pizza.
- Place the pizza on the lower rack. If you have an accessory pack, you could place the pizza on the browning tray – otherwise, place it directly on the rack or use a pizza tray.
- You may want to place the upper rack upside down on the top of the pizza for the first 10 minutes. This prevents the toppings from lifting with the force of the fan and it is more advisable if your pizza has lots of loose toppings. The Flavorwave Turbo Platinum has three fan settings so, alternatively, you could opt for a low fan setting which will avoid the need to cover the top of the pizza.
- Set the temperature to 220–240°C and cook for 10–15 minutes until golden.

# Frozen Oven Chips

If you have children or teenagers in the house, there will come a time when they want you to cook some oven chips. The halogen oven cooks these in approximately 20 minutes.

- Turn the halogen oven to 220°C.
- Place the oven chips on a baking tray on the low rack.
- I sprinkle them with a touch of paprika and a tiny dash of olive oil to add flavour and to prevent the chips from becoming too dry.
- Cook for 20–25 minutes, turning occasionally if you feel like it, until they are golden. If you use a browning tray, the chips should brown all over.

# Fresh Waffles topped with Mozzarella, Pancetta and Sundried Tomatoes

A really simple snack everyone will enjoy!

- Preheat the halogen oven using the preheat setting or set the temperature to the highest available.
- Place the waffles and pancetta on the high rack and grill for a few minutes either side until they are cooked.
- Remove and spread some pesto on the waffles.
- Stack the waffles with the mozzarella, pancetta and sundried tomatoes and place back on the high rack for 2–3 minutes to help melt the mozzarella.
- Season to taste and serve with a little side salad and homemade relish.

4 fresh waffles
4–6 rashers of
   pancetta
4–6 teaspoons pesto
1 ball of mozzarella,
   torn
6–8 sundried tomatoes
   (drained from oil)
Seasoning to taste

# Toasted Cheese and Ham Croissants

**SERVES 4**

4 croissants
Mature cheddar
4–6 slices of ham
Seasoning to taste

As with the panini, bruschetta, waffles and toasted sandwiches, these recipes are designed to show you what you can do with the halogen. Feel free to change the ingredients to suit your palate. Why not try a sweet filling. One of my children's favourites is chocolate spread with slices of banana.

- Preheat the halogen oven using the preheat setting or set the temperature to the highest available.
- Slice the croissants in half and fill with cheese and ham.
- Place the filled croissants on the high rack and cook for 3–6 minutes until crispy and the cheese starts to melt.
- Serve immediately.

# Crumpets

There is nothing like the taste of hot, buttered crumpets. You could add some crumbled stilton for a savoury variation – yummy!

- Preheat the halogen oven using the preheat setting or turn the temperature to the highest setting once you are ready to grill.
- Place the crumpets on the high rack and grill until they reach your desired toasting.
- If you want to add a topping, do so after the crumpets have started to brown and not at the beginning of the process.
- Serve hot.

# Potatoes

Jacket potatoes are delicious and in terms of running costs this is where a halogen cooker excels over a conventional oven. Depending on their size, jacket potatoes can be made in 40–60 minutes and, unlike cooking them in a microwave, they have a crispy skin with a delicious fluffy middle. Baked potatoes can be topped with leftover chilli, bolognese, curry, grated cheese, tuna or even humble baked beans.

Some people rub a little sea salt into the skins before baking – others brush with olive oil to help crisp up the skins. It is personal preference, so I will leave this aspect up to you!

SERVES 4

4 large potatoes
Knob of butter
100g mature cheddar,
   grated
1–2 carrots, grated
Dash of
   Worcestershire sauce
Black pepper to taste

# Cheesy Jackets

With a little imagination, jacket toppings can be so much more than a bit of grated cheese or some tuna. Here is a simple suggestion to spice up the popular cheesy jacket.

- Preheat the halogen oven using the preheat setting or set the temperature to 200°C.
- Select your potatoes and prick them all over with a sharp knife. Place them on the low rack.
- Bake the potatoes until they are soft in the middle but the jackets are crunchy. This normally takes around 45–60 minutes, depending on size.
- Cut the jackets in half, scoop out the middles and place the potato in a large bowl. Return the empty jackets to the oven for 5 minutes to crisp.
- Meanwhile, mix the potato with the butter, cheese, carrots, Worcestershire sauce and black pepper.
- Re-stuff the jackets and finish with a sprinkling of grated cheese on top.
- Bake for another 5 minutes until the tops are golden. Delicious!

There are many possible variations to this recipe. The formula remains the same – scoop out the middle of the baked potato and mix the ingredients together, then place it back in the oven to brown. Here are some more suggestions.

SUITABLE FOR VEGETARIANS

# Italian Jackets

- Preheat the halogen oven using the preheat setting or set the temperature to 200°C.
- Select your potatoes and prick them all over with a sharp knife. Place them on the low rack.
- Bake the potatoes until they are soft in the middle but the jackets are crunchy. This normally takes around 45–60 minutes, depending on size.
- Once the potatoes are cooked, cut them in half and scoop out the middles. Mix the potato with the butter, cheese, pancetta and oregano. Add a dash of milk if the mixture is too dry (it should be the consistency of mashed potato). Season to taste.
- Re-stuff the jackets and finish with a sprinkling of grated cheese on top.
- Bake for another 5 minutes until the tops are golden.

4 potatoes
25g butter
150g Gorgonzola cheese, crumbled
150g pancetta, chopped
1 teaspoon oregano
Dash of milk
Seasoning to taste

# Sour Cream and Chive Jackets

4 potatoes
100g sour cream
1 tablespoon chives,
   freshly chopped
50g mature cheddar,
   grated (optional)
Seasoning to taste

- Preheat the halogen oven using the preheat setting or set the temperature to 200°C.
- Select your potatoes and prick them all over with a sharp knife. Place them on the low rack.
- Bake the potatoes until they are soft in the middle but the jackets are crunchy. This normally takes around 45–60 minutes, depending on size.
- Once the potatoes are cooked, cut them in half and scoop out the middles. Mix the potato with the sour cream and chives. Season to taste.
- Re-stuff the jackets and finish with a sprinkling of grated cheese on top.
- Bake for another 5 minutes until the tops are golden.

SUITABLE FOR VEGETARIANS

# Love–Hate Jackets

This recipe is so named because most people seem to fall into one of two groups: those who love Marmite and those who hate it!

4 potatoes
Knob of butter or vegan margarine
4 teaspoons Marmite or yeast extract
75g mature cheddar, grated (vegans can omit the cheese or opt for a vegan cheese alternative)
Dash of milk or soya milk

- Preheat the halogen oven using the preheat setting or set the temperature to 200°C.
- Select your potatoes and prick them all over with a sharp knife. Place them on the low rack.
- Bake the potatoes until they are soft in the middle but the jackets are crunchy. This normally takes around 45–60 minutes, depending on size.
- Once the potatoes are cooked, cut them in half and scoop out the middles. Mix the potato with the butter, Marmite and cheese. Add a dash of milk if the mixture is too dry (it should be the consistency of mashed potato).
- Re-stuff the jackets and finish with a sprinkling of grated cheese on top.
- Bake for another 5 minutes in the oven until the tops are golden.

SUITABLE FOR VEGETARIANS OR VEGANS

# Egg in the Nest Jackets

SERVES 4

4 large potatoes
Knob of butter
50–75g mature
  cheddar
2 teaspoons chopped
  chives
Dash of milk
4 eggs
Seasoning to taste

- Preheat the halogen oven using the preheat setting or set the temperature to 200°C.
- Select your potatoes and prick them all over with a sharp knife. Place them on the low rack.
- Bake the potatoes until they are soft in the middle but the jackets are crunchy. This normally takes around 45–60 minutes, depending on size.
- Once the potatoes are cooked, cut them in half and scoop out the middles. Mix the potato with the butter, cheese and chives. Add a dash of milk if the mixture is too dry (it should be the consistency of mashed potato). Season to taste.
- Re-stuff the jackets. Using a spoon, make a hollow in the middle of each potato, large enough to fit in the egg. Break an egg into 4 of the potato halves, leaving 4 with just the cheese mixture.
- Bake for a further 10–12 minutes until the eggs are firm and the tops are golden.

# Tuna and Mayo Jackets

SERVES 4

- Preheat the halogen oven using the preheat setting or set the temperature to 200°C.
- Select your potatoes and prick them all over with a sharp knife. Place them on the low rack.
- Bake the potatoes until they are soft in the middle but the jackets are crunchy. This normally takes around 45–60 minutes, depending on size.
- Once the potatoes are cooked, cut them in half and scoop out the middles. Mix the potato with the butter, mayo, tuna and sweetcorn and mix thoroughly. Add a dash of milk if the mixture is too dry (it should be the consistency of mashed potato). Season to taste.
- Re-stuff the jackets and finish with a sprinkling of grated cheese on top.
- Bake in the oven for another 5 minutes until the tops are golden.

4 potatoes
Knob of butter
1–2 large dollops of mayonnaise
1 tin tuna, mashed
50g sweetcorn (optional)
Dash of milk
Seasoning to taste
Grated cheese (optional)

4 sweet potatoes,
   scrubbed
30–50g mature
   cheddar
Seasoning to taste
Dash of milk

# Baked Sweet Potato

If you have never tasted a baked sweet potato, I urge you to try one – they really are delicious. I love adding a little bit of grated cheese and serving with a portion of baked beans. A really simple meal but very wholesome and healthy! Why not look at the baked potato recipes in this chapter and use sweet potatoes instead or create your own recipe.

- Preheat the halogen oven using the preheat setting or set the temperature to 200°C.
- Select your potatoes and prick them all over with a sharp knife. Place them on the low rack.
- Bake the potatoes until they are soft in the middle but the jackets are crunchy. This normally takes around 45–60 minutes, depending on size.
- Once the potatoes are cooked, cut them in half and scoop out the middles. Mix the potato with the cheese and seasoning. Add a dash of milk if the mixture is too dry (it should be the consistency of mashed potato).
- Re-stuff the jackets. Bake in the oven for 10–12 minutes until the tops are golden.

SUITABLE FOR VEGETARIANS

# Baked New Potatoes

This must be the simplest recipe of all!

- Preheat the oven using the preheat setting or set the temperature to 220°C.
- Place the potatoes in the halogen bowl with the olive oil, garlic, herbs and paprika. Stir well, ensuring the potatoes are all coated. This will give them a vibrant red/gold colour.
- Bake in the oven for approximately 35–45 minutes until golden. Simple!

SUITABLE FOR VEGETARIANS AND VEGANS

SERVES 4

1kg bag of new potatoes, washed
Dash of olive oil
2–3 cloves garlic, crushed
2–3 teaspoons mixed herbs (fresh or dried)
2–3 teaspoons paprika
Seasoning to taste

4–6 large potatoes,
  peeled and cut to
  size
Oil of your choice (I
  use olive or
  sunflower oil)
3–4 teaspoons
  semolina
2–3 teaspoons paprika

# Delicious Roast Potatoes

*Who can resist a roast potato!*

- Preheat the halogen oven using the preheat setting or set the temperature to 220°C.
- Peel and cut the potatoes ready to roast.
- Steam or boil the potatoes for 10 minutes. While the potatoes are cooking, add the oil (about 2cm in depth) to a roasting tin and place on the low rack. Alternatively, you can add the oil to the base of the halogen oven but, as air does not circulate on the base, cooking times will need to be increased.
- Drain the potatoes and return them to the saucepan.
- Sprinkle the semolina and paprika onto the potatoes. Put the lid on the pan and shake the potatoes for a few seconds.
- Add the potatoes to the hot roasting oil, being careful not to splash.
- Roast for 50–60 minutes (more if they are larger potatoes), turning regularly to ensure an even, crisp coating. When you turn the potatoes, add more paprika.

SUITABLE FOR VEGETARIANS AND VEGANS

# Garlic and Rosemary Roast Potatoes

These have a fantastic flavour.

SERVES 4

- Preheat the halogen oven using the preheat setting or set the temperature to 220°C.
- Peel and cut the potatoes ready to roast.
- Steam or boil the potatoes for 10 minutes. While the potatoes are cooking, add the oil or goose fat (about 2cm in depth) to a roasting tin and place on the low rack.
- Drain the potatoes and return them to the saucepan.
- Sprinkle the semolina onto the potatoes. Put the lid on the pan and shake the potatoes for a few seconds.
- Add the potatoes to the hot roasting oil, being careful not to splash. Add the garlic cloves, onion wedges and rosemary leaves, ensuring they are evenly distributed over the potatoes.
- Roast for 50–60 minutes (more if they are larger potatoes), turning regularly to ensure an even, crisp coating.

SUITABLE FOR VEGETARIANS AND VEGANS

4–6 large potatoes, peeled and cut to size
Olive oil or goose fat
3–4 teaspoons of semolina
1 bulb of garlic (with the cloves separated and peeled)
1–2 red onions, cut into wedges
3–5 sprigs of rosemary

# Potato Wedges

4–6 potatoes, cut into
  chunks
1 tablespoon olive oil
1–2 teaspoons paprika

Don't waste your money on horrible frozen potato wedges –
try making your own. Not only are they cheaper, they taste so
much nicer.

- Preheat the halogen oven using the preheat setting or
  set the temperature to 230–240°C.
- Place the potato chunks in a bowl with the olive oil
  and paprika, ensuring the potatoes are evenly coated.
- Transfer the potatoes to a baking tray or simply place
  them on the bottom of the halogen.
- Cook for 25–30 minutes until golden, turning
  occasionally.

*Variations:* Add chopped garlic, chillies or herbs of your
choice for extra taste.

SUITABLE FOR VEGETARIANS AND VEGANS

# Cheese Crunch New Potatoes

These are really yummy – but be warned, they are quite addictive.

- Steam the new potatoes, still in their skins, until tender.
- While the potatoes are steaming, mix the garlic, parmesan, dried onion, chives and olive oil together. Season to taste.
- Preheat the halogen oven using the preheat setting or turn the temperature to 200°C.
- Place the potatoes on a lightly oiled ovenproof dish, making sure this fits in your halogen.
- Using a potato masher, very gently push down on each potato to slightly flatten it. Place a small amount of the cheesy mixture onto each potato.
- Place the potatoes on the low rack and cook for 15–20 minutes until golden.

SUITABLE FOR VEGETARIANS AND VEGANS

1kg new potatoes
2–3 cloves of garlic, crushed
30–40g grated parmesan
1–2 tablespoons dried onion
1 teaspoon dried chives
2–3 tablespoons olive oil
Seasoning to taste

# Fan Potatoes

SERVES 4

4–6 medium or large potatoes
2–3 cloves garlic, crushed
4 teaspoons butter (or, if vegan, a dairy-free spread)
2–3 teaspoons paprika
1–2 teaspoons mixed herbs
Seasoning to taste
Drizzle of olive oil

These are a great favourite with my dad and make a good alternative to roast or jacket potatoes. You can coat them with any herbs or spices and they are lovely with fresh chillies – this recipe is more restrained and uses mixed herbs and garlic.

- Preheat the halogen oven using the preheat setting or set the temperature to 210°C.
- Select your potatoes and wash but don't peel them. Place them on a chopping board and, using a sharp knife, cut thin slices into the top two thirds of each potato, stopping one third up from the base so that the potato remains intact.  Slice all of the potatoes in this way.
- Rub butter over the top of the potatoes, pushing a little between the slices if you can without breaking them.
- Sprinkle with garlic, followed by paprika and mixed herbs. Season to taste.
- Place the potatoes on a baking tray and drizzle with a little olive oil – not too much!
- Place on the low rack and cook for 20 minutes. As the potatoes cook, they will open out slightly. If you want each slice to golden, add a little more butter or herbs half way through cooking.
- Lower the temperature to 180°C and cook for another 25–30 minutes until golden.

SUITABLE FOR VEGETARIANS AND VEGANS

# Cheesy Dauphine Potatoes

SERVES 4

A classic dish that never fails to impress. If you are not concerned about calories, you could opt for cream instead of crème fraîche.

500g potatoes, very
  finely sliced
2 cloves of garlic,
  crushed
400ml crème fraîche
150ml milk
Pinch of grated
  nutmeg
Seasoning to taste
75g Gruyère cheese,
  grated

- Preheat the halogen oven using the preheat setting or set the temperature to 200°C.
- In a bowl, mix the garlic, crème fraîche and milk until combined thoroughly. Season with nutmeg, salt and pepper.
- Grease an ovenproof dish, and then start to make layers of potato slices followed by a little grated cheese. Place a little of the crème fraîche mixture between each layer, leaving the majority to pour over the top layer.
- Continue making layers, finishing with the crème fraîche and a little grated cheese and black pepper.
- Place in the oven on the low rack and cook for 50–60 minutes, until the potatoes are cooked. If the top starts to look too cooked, cover the dish with tin foil.

SUITABLE FOR VEGETARIANS

# Cheesy Mash, Egg and Tomato Pie

4–5 potatoes, mashed
30g butter
100g mature cheddar, grated
Seasoning to taste
4 eggs
150g oats
150g breadcrumbs
30g dried onion
50g parmesan cheese
4 tomatoes, sliced

I found this recipe in an old 1920's book and have adapted it to suit our tastes. It works perfectly in the halogen oven – although it's a good idea to remember to cook double the amount of mashed potato the night before to have it ready for making this dish.

- Cook and mash the potato. Add the butter and the cheddar and season to taste.
- Preheat the halogen oven using the preheat setting or set the temperature to 210°C.
- Grease an ovenproof dish before adding the mashed potato. Break the eggs onto the potato.
- Mix the oats, breadcrumbs, dried onion and parmesan cheese together. Season to taste.
- Cover the eggs with a layer of the breadcrumb mix. Add a layer of sliced tomato and finish with another layer of breadcrumbs. Add a couple of small dollops of butter.
- Place on the low rack and cook for 20–25 minutes until golden.

SUITABLE FOR VEGETARIANS

# Potato, Cheese and Spring Onion Tortilla

This is an ideal dish for using up any leftover cooked potatoes.

- Preheat the halogen oven using the preheat setting or set the temperature to 200°C.
- In a large bowl, beat the eggs well. Add the remaining ingredients and combine.
- Pour this mixture onto a well-greased ovenproof dish.
- Place on the low rack and cook for 20–25 minutes until firm.
- Serve hot or cold with salad.

SUITABLE FOR VEGETARIANS

SERVES 4

5 eggs
1 bunch of spring onions, finely chopped
2–3 medium potatoes, cooked and sliced or cubed
50–75g mature cheese (e.g. cheddar or parmesan)
1 teaspoon thyme (optional)
Seasoning to taste

3–4 large potatoes,
  sliced into chips
Olive oil spray
Paprika (optional)
Sea salt

# Homemade Golden Chips

Who can resist chips? These are made using spray oil so that you can cut down on the amount of fat, making it a guilt-free indulgence. (I place olive oil in a disused spray container as it is cheaper than buying readymade spray oils.)

- Preheat the halogen oven using the preheat setting or set the temperature to 220°C.
- Place the sliced potatoes in a bowl of water for a few minutes. Drain and steam or boil for 5 minutes.
- Meanwhile, spray the baking tray with olive oil. I use the browning tray for this as it helps to brown the chips all over. Drain the potatoes and place on the baking tray in a single layer. Spray with a little more olive oil and sprinkle with paprika (this is optional but it helps to create a golden colour and nice flavour).
- Place on the low rack and bake for 10–15 minutes. Then turn the chips over, spray them again and bake for another 10–15 minutes or until they are cooked. The cooking times depend on the thickness of your chips.
- To serve, sprinkle with sea salt.

SUITABLE FOR VEGETARIANS AND VEGANS

# Homemade Sweet Potato Chips

SERVES 4

- Preheat the halogen oven using the preheat setting or set the temperature to 220°C.
- Steam or boil the sliced potatoes for 5 minutes.
- Meanwhile, spray the baking tray with olive oil. I use the browning tray for this as it helps to brown the chips all over. Drain the potatoes and place on the baking tray in a single layer. Spray with a little more olive oil and sprinkle with paprika (this is optional but it helps to create a golden colour and nice flavour).
- Place on the low rack and bake for 10–15 minutes. Then turn the chips over, spray them again and add the chilli flakes. Cook for another 10–15 minutes or until they are cooked. The cooking times depend on the thickness of your chips.
- To serve, sprinkle with sea salt and more chilli flakes if preferred.

SUITABLE FOR VEGETARIANS AND VEGANS

3–4 large sweet potatoes, sliced into chips
Olive oil spray
Paprika (optional)
Fresh or dried chilli flakes
Sea salt

# Meat

The halogen oven can cook meat slightly quicker than the conventional oven, though you have to be careful to get your temperature settings right. Too high and the tops of the joints or bird will burn whilst the middle may remain raw or undercooked. I would advise using a temperature gauge to test your meat, particularly poultry or joints of meat, until you are more confident – even when following a recipe.

When meat is placed on the lower rack, it allows the juices and fats to drain away therefore making the meat healthier. Some people worry that the meat will dry out too much but, to be honest, meat does tend to be very tender and moist when cooked in the halogen oven – unless you overcook it! If you are concerned, you can always place your meat on a baking tray or even cook on the base of the halogen cooker – ideal if you also want to roast potatoes.

You can cook a joint as you would in a conventional oven – roughly 20 minutes per 500g at 180°C and add another 10 minutes to the end of the cooking time.

As with all foods cooked in the halogen oven, make sure there is adequate space between the element and the food – ideally at least 2–3cm. The nearer the food is to the element, the more likely it is to burn or cook quickly. If you are concerned, wrap some foil over the food for the first half of the cooking time, though make sure it is secured well as it can be lifted by the power of the fan.

**SERVES 4–6**

1 whole chicken
1 red onion
1 lemon
30g butter
1–2 teaspoons
tarragon

# Roast Chicken

Chicken is the nation's favourite and this is a great way to cook your Sunday roast. Don't forget to add your roast potatoes (choose one of the recipes from Chapter 3).

- Preheat the halogen oven using the preheat setting or turn the temperature to 240°C.
- Wash and prepare the chicken according to your own preference. I place a whole red onion and a lemon, both cut in half, in the cavity of the bird to enhance its flavour. I then rub the skin with butter and sprinkle with herbs, or you can place herb butter under the skin.
- Place the chicken, breast side down, on the lower rack for 25 minutes.
- Turn the chicken back over so the breast side is up, reduce the temperature to 210°C and cook for another 40 minutes until cooked – the cooking time obviously depends on the size of the bird. As with all meats, make sure the meat is thoroughly cooked before eating.
- The fat will have drained to the base of the halogen oven – you can use some of this juice to make your gravy.

# Roast Beef with Horseradish

SERVES 4–6

A great family roast. Serve with roast potatoes, Yorkshire puddings, steamed vegetables and homemade gravy.

Beef joint
2 tablespoons dark brown sugar
2 tablespoons maple or golden syrup
4 tablespoons horseradish
Black pepper
300ml red wine

- Preheat the halogen oven using the preheat setting or set the temperature to 210°C.
- In a mixing bowl, combine the sugar, syrup and horseradish. Season well with black pepper.
- Place the beef joint in a roasting tin and place on the low rack. Cook for 20 minutes and then turn down the temperature to 180°C.
- Coat well with the sticky horseradish sauce and cook for a further 20 minutes for every 450g. If the meat starts to darken too much whilst cooking, cover it securely with tin foil.
- Halfway through cooking add the red wine – it will mix with the beef juices and can be used for your beef gravy stock.
- Once cooked, wrap the joint in tin foil and leave it to rest for at least 20 minutes. Use this time to make your gravy. Simply combine the meat's natural juices from the roasting pan with a little cornflour to help thicken them up.
- Serve with roast potatoes, Yorkshire puddings and steamed vegetables.

# Roast Leg of Lamb with Roasted Vegetables

A great roast or one-pot-meal.

1 leg of lamb

3–4 cloves of garlic, crushed

½ teaspoon chillies, chopped

1 teaspoon dried rosemary

2–3 tablespoons olive oil

Seasoning to taste

2 sweet potatoes

6–8 potatoes

2–3 teaspoons paprika

2–3 teaspoons semolina

2 red onions

2–3 tablespoons olive oil

2–3 sprigs of fresh rosemary

- Preheat the halogen oven using the preheat settings or set the temperature to 230°C.
- Mix together the garlic, chilli, dried rosemary, olive oil and seasoning to form a paste. Rub this over the leg of lamb. You can score the flesh first to help give the paste something to hold on to.
- Place on the lower rack and cook for 15 minutes.
- Meanwhile, cut the potatoes to size and steam or parboil them for 10 minutes. Drain and then return them to the empty saucepan. Add the paprika and semolina.  Pop the lid back on the saucepan and shake to fluff up and coat the vegetables.
- Place the potatoes around the lamb and brush them with olive oil. Cut the onions in half and place them with the vegetables, along with the sprigs of rosemary.
- Cook for another 10 minutes at 230°C. Then reduce the temperature to 180°C and cook for another 30–45 minutes or until both the meat and potatoes are cooked to your satisfaction. (Exact cooking times depend on the size of the joint.) Remember to turn the lamb and vegetables regularly and add a brush of oil or paste as required.

# Stuffed Loin of Pork

A great family roast – serve it with roast potatoes, vegetables and homemade gravy.

- Preheat the halogen oven using the preheat setting or set the temperature to 210°C.
- In a mixing bowl, add the breadcrumbs, onion, garlic, bacon, pine nuts, sundried tomatoes and chopped herbs. Combine well and season to taste.
- Place the stuffing on the meat and roll tightly. Use water-soaked string to tie the loin securely.
- Rub the skin with olive oil and sprinkle with sea salt and black pepper.
- Place the loin on a baking or roasting tray on the low rack, or directly on the rack if you want the juices to drain. Cook for 20 minutes. Then turn down the temperature to 180°C and cook for 30 minutes for every 500g. If the meat starts to darken too much whilst cooking, cover it securely with tin foil. Use a meat thermometer to check that the meat is cooked, or check the juices – if they are running clear, it should be cooked.
- Leave the meat to rest for 10–15 minutes before carving.

75g breadcrumbs
1 red onion, finely chopped
2–3 cloves of garlic, finely chopped
Half a pack of lean bacon, chopped
50g pine nuts
6–8 sundried tomatoes (in oil), chopped
Handful of fresh herbs (sage, thyme, oregano or parsley), chopped
Seasoning to taste
Loin of pork
Olive oil
Sea salt
Black pepper

# Chicken Burgers

SERVES 4

1 onion, chopped
1–2 cloves garlic,
   crushed
1 stick of celery,
   chopped
½ yellow pepper,
   chopped
500g chicken mince
30g pine nuts
1 tablespoon home-
   prepared, wholemeal
   breadcrumbs

*Forget fast food restaurants – why not make your own?*

- Place all the ingredients in a food processor and mix thoroughly.
- When mixed, form into balls – these should be firm but moist. If the mixture is dry, add some beaten egg.
- Use the palm of your hand to flatten the balls into burger shapes. Refrigerate them until you are ready to use them, or freeze in layers (separate each layer with parchment to prevent them from sticking together).
- When you are ready to cook the burgers, brush the meat lightly with olive oil. Turn the halogen oven to 250°C, place the burgers on the high rack and cook for 4–5 minutes on each side until golden. (You are actually grilling them at this heat!)
- Serve with wholemeal baps, a salad garnish and a dollop of mayonnaise.

# Cheat's Leftover Chicken Pie

This is my mum's recipe. Now we have grown up and flown the nest, Mum and Dad have had to adapt to cooking for two instead of four. This meal is made from the leftovers of Mum's Sunday roast, so they usually tuck into it early in the week.

- Heat the oil in a pan and fry the onion. Add the celery, mushrooms, cooked chicken and ham if you are using it. Cook for 3–4 minutes.
- Add the soup and heat for a further 3 minutes.
- Place the mixture in an ovenproof pie dish, first making sure it fits in your halogen oven.
- Roll out the pastry to a size larger than required. Wet the edges of the pie dish with milk or water. Cut thin strips of pastry and place them around the edge of the pie dish. Dampen again with milk. This will give the top pastry something to hold on to. Cut the top pastry to size and place over the pie. Crimp and seal the edges thoroughly.
- Place on the low rack and set the temperature to 200°C. Cook for 20–30 minutes until the pie crust is golden.

Drizzle or spray of olive oil
1 onion, chopped
2 sticks of celery, chopped
75g mushrooms, quartered
200–300g cooked chicken, removed from the bone
100g cooked ham (optional)
1 can of chicken or mushroom condensed soup
Half a pack of readymade puff pastry

1 onion, finely
chopped
2–3 cloves garlic,
crushed
1 teaspoon coriander
powder
1 teaspoon cayenne
pepper
1 teaspoon chilli
powder (or fresh
chillies, finely
chopped)
1 teaspoon curry
powder
2 teaspoons turmeric
2–3 teaspoons paprika
2½cm (1in) knuckle of
ginger, grated
Juice and zest of 1
lemon
Dash of olive oil
100g low fat natural
yoghurt
4 large pieces of
chicken (or you can
use any leftover
chicken)

# Tandoori Chicken

You can cheat with this recipe and use a tandoori paste.
However, I prefer to make it myself – there is something deeply
satisfying about flinging around herbs and spices when
cooking, and it is a great way to get the family's attention as
the flavours start to waft around the house.

- In an ovenproof dish, mix the onion, garlic, herbs
  and spices with the lemon juice, zest, olive oil and
  yoghurt.
- Add the chicken pieces and combine thoroughly. For
  the best flavour, leave to marinate for a few hours.
- When you are ready, preheat your halogen oven using
  the preheat setting or set the temperature to 200°C.
- Place the chicken and the marinade in an ovenproof
  dish. Place on the low rack and cook for 20–25
  minutes.
- Serve on a bed of rice.

# Chicken Italiano

The flavours of this dish are delightful. There is a veggie version of this recipe in Chapter 6.

- In a large sauté pan, fry the onion and garlic in a dash of olive oil for 2 minutes. Add the red pepper and cook for another 2 minutes.
- Add the chicken, pancetta or bacon and paprika. Stir, cooking gently for 5 minutes.
- Add all the remaining ingredients. Cook for another couple of minutes.
- Pour this into a casserole dish that fits in the halogen oven. Cover the pan with a lid and cook at 180°C for 35–40 minutes.
- Serve with small roast or sauté potatoes and vegetables.

**SERVES 4**

Dash of olive oil
1 onion
2–3 cloves garlic, crushed
1 red pepper, diced
4 chicken breasts, fillets or pieces
3–4 rashers of pancetta or bacon, diced
2 teaspoons paprika
1 tin of chopped tomatoes
2 teaspoons sundried tomato paste
200ml red wine
200ml stock or water
150g button mushrooms
Small handful of fresh basil, chopped
Seasoning to taste

# Chicken and Mushroom Casserole

*A wholesome meal that everyone loves.*

A drizzle or spray of olive oil
1–2 cloves garlic
2 leeks, finely chopped
6 spring onions, finely chopped
300g chicken pieces (you can use cooked chicken)
175g mushrooms
200ml white wine
300ml chicken stock
1 teaspoon cornflour
1 teaspoon paprika
100g French beans
1 teaspoon dried tarragon (or a handful of fresh tarragon)

• Heat a little olive oil in a sauté pan and cook the garlic, leeks and spring onions for 2–3 minutes. Add the chicken and the mushrooms and cook for a further 5 minutes.
• Place the chicken mixture in a casserole dish, first making sure it fits in the halogen oven. Add the wine and stock to the dish.
• Mix the cornflour with 10ml of water in a cup to form a smooth paste and then add to the chicken pot.
• Add all the remaining ingredients. If you are using fresh tarragon, add half now and retain half to add in the last 10 minutes of cooking.
• Cook at 180°C for 35–40 minutes. If the casserole starts to form a skin on the top you can pop on the casserole lid, or wrap securely a piece of tin foil over the top of the dish.

*Note:* If you prefer a creamier sauce, add some low fat Greek yoghurt or low fat crème fraîche 5 minutes before serving.

# Sticky Chicken Drumsticks

*They are finger licking good!*

SERVES 4

3 tablespoons maple syrup or honey
1 tablespoon mustard
1 tablespoon Worcestershire sauce
1 tablespoon soy sauce
2 teaspoons paprika
4 chicken drumsticks

- Place all the ingredients apart from the chicken in a bowl and mix well.
- Score the drumsticks with a sharp knife to give the marinade something to hold on to.
- Have a large freezer bag ready – this can get messy! Place the drumsticks in the freezer bag with the marinade and shake well to ensure they are thoroughly coated. Secure and leave in the fridge overnight.
- When you are ready to cook, place a baking tray under the high rack to catch any drips. Turn the oven on to 230°C.
- Place the drumsticks on the high rack. You can place them directly onto the rack or, if you prefer, use a baking tray.
- Cook the chicken gently on both sides, adding marinade as you go if you prefer. The advantage of cooking the chicken straight on the rack is the oven's ability to cook all sides, but you will still need to turn the drumsticks over to get an even browning. Cook until the chicken is thoroughly cooked – this should take about 15–20 minutes depending on the size of the drumsticks.
- Serve with salad.

3–4 sirloin steaks
2–3 cloves of garlic
Dash of olive oil
Black pepper to
  season

# Grilled Steak

A quick and easy meal served with a delicious salad.

- Prepare your steaks as you would normally do. I rub mine with garlic and olive oil and season with black pepper.
- Place on the high rack, either directly on the rack or on a browning plate if you have one.
- Set the temperature to 240°C and cook for 8–10 minutes. Reduce or increase the temperature to achieve your desired taste – this timing is perfect for a medium rare, 2–3cm thick steak.

# Beef Burgers

Forget the fast food chains – your own homemade burgers not only taste superior, they are also much healthier.

- Put the onion and garlic into a large bowl and stir well. Add the beef and breadcrumbs and mix thoroughly.
- Add the beaten egg, coriander, cumin, mustard and tomato purée. Season to taste.
- Mix thoroughly and form into balls – these should be firm but moist. Use the palm of your hand to flatten the balls into burger shapes.
- Place the burgers in the fridge until you are ready to use them, or freeze them in layers (separate the layers with parchment to prevent them from sticking together). When you are ready to cook them, brush them lightly with olive oil. Turn the halogen oven to 250°C. Place them on the high rack and cook for 5–8 minutes on each side until golden. (You are actually grilling them at this heat!)
- Garnish with salad and serve with wholemeal baps.

*Variation:* If you like them slightly spicy, why not add some chopped chillies and 1 teaspoon of curry powder to the burger ingredients before mixing. You could also brush the burgers with chilli oil instead of olive oil to add a tasty zing.

SERVES 4

1 onion, finely chopped
1 clove of garlic, crushed
400g lean beef mince
1 tablespoon home-prepared wholemeal breadcrumbs
1 egg, beaten
1 teaspoon coriander
1 teaspoon cumin
1 teaspoon yellow mustard
2 teaspoons tomato purée
Seasoning to taste

# Lamb and Apricot Casserole

A lovely lamb casserole with a small kick to liven things up.

**SERVES 4–6**

A drizzle or spray of olive oil

1 onion, chopped

2–3 cloves of garlic, crushed

400g lamb, diced

3 teaspoons harissa paste or hot chilli paste

2 teaspoons cinnamon powder

200ml red wine

1 tin chopped tomatoes

300-400ml hot water or stock

1 tin chickpeas, drained

75g dried apricots, chopped

Fresh coriander leaves to garnish

- Heat the oil in a sauté or frying pan and cook the onion, garlic and lamb for 2–3 minutes.
- Add the harissa paste and stir well for 2 minutes.
- Turn the halogen oven to 200°C. Select your casserole dish, making sure it fits comfortably in your oven.
- Place the lamb mixture in the casserole dish. Add all the remaining ingredients and combine well. Pop on the casserole lid or cover securely with tin foil.
- Place on the low rack and cook for 50 minutes.
- Serve, garnished with coriander leaves.

# Cashew, Walnut and Mushroom Stuffed Chicken

SERVES 4

A really simple dish to prepare, but it tastes fabulous!

- Preheat the halogen oven using the preheat setting or turn the temperature to 200°C.
- Using a food processor is the best and quickest way to make this dish. Use it to chop the cashew nuts, walnuts, mushrooms and onion. Place these chopped ingredients in a bowl and mix in the garlic.
- Combine well and add the marmite, mixing to ensure it is evenly distributed.
- With a sharp knife, cut a slit in the side of each chicken breast to form a pocket. Stuff the mixture into these pockets. Then wrap each breast in pancetta to secure them.
- Place the chicken breasts on a greased ovenproof dish. Drizzle with a little oil and season to taste.
- Place on the low rack and cook for 30–35 minutes until the chicken is cooked.

30g cashew nuts
30g walnuts
125g chestnut
    mushrooms
1 onion
2–3 cloves of garlic
½–1 teaspoon marmite
4 chicken breasts
8 rashers of pancetta
Olive oil
Seasoning to taste

400g lamb, cubed
50g plain flour
2–3 teaspoons paprika
Olive oil
3–4 leeks, sliced
2 cloves of garlic,
  crushed
1–2 carrots, chopped
Knob of butter
500ml lamb stock
1 teaspoon mixed
  herbs
2–3 sprigs of fresh
  thyme (or cube of
  frozen fresh thyme)
6–8 potatoes, thinly
  sliced
25g mature cheddar,
  grated

# Lamb Hotpot

*A family favourite.*

- In a bowl mix the lamb with the flour and paprika, ensuring the lamb is evenly coated all over.
- Heat a little olive oil in a large sauté pan and fry the leeks and garlic for 2–3 minutes. Add the meat, carrots and butter and cook for a further 2–3 minutes to brown the meat.
- Pour on the stock, dried herbs and thyme and cook for 10 minutes.
- Place a layer of potato slices in the bottom of a greased casserole dish, first making sure it fits inside your halogen oven. Cover with a layer of the meat mixture and continue alternating layers of meat and potato, finishing with a final layer of potato slices. Pop on a lid or cover securely with tin foil.
- Turn on the halogen oven to 210°C. Place the casserole dish on the low rack and cook for 45 minutes.
- Remove from the oven and sprinkle over the grated cheese. Then return the hotpot to the oven without a lid for a final 20–25 minutes until the potatoes are tender.

# Red Pesto Chicken Parcels

SERVES 4

Such simplicity! If you want to include some roast or mini roast potatoes, choose a recipe from Chapter 3.

- Preheat the halogen oven using the preheat setting or turn on to 200°C.
- Cut out four squares of foil, twice the size of each chicken breast. Grease each one with a little butter.
- Place one chicken breast in the middle of each square. Add 1–2 teaspoons of red pesto to each chicken breast. Cover with some onion slices.
- Drizzle with a tablespoon of white wine. Season well and secure into a parcel.
- Place on the low rack and cook for 30–35 minutes until the chicken is cooked.

4 chicken breasts
Butter
4–8 teaspoons of red
   pesto
1 red onion, sliced
4 tablespoons of white
   wine
Seasoning

1–2 chillies, finely chopped

2 cloves of garlic, finely chopped

2–3 teaspoons chilli sauce (mild or hot depending on your taste)

Juice and zest of 1 lemon

1 teaspoon paprika

1 teaspoon allspice

½ teaspoon ginger

½ teaspoon chilli powder

1 tablespoon brown sugar

2 teaspoons maple syrup or 3 teaspoons honey

10–12 chicken wings

Seasoning to taste

# Spicy Chicken Wings

A really simple dish that takes minutes to prepare. Marinate overnight or for at least one hour before cooking in the oven. Serve with rice and salad for a great summer evening, alfresco supper.

- In a bowl, combine all the ingredients apart from the chicken wings.
- Then add the chicken wings to the bowl, ensuring they are thoroughly coated with the mixture. Cover with cling film and leave to marinate overnight or for at least 1 hour. (If the bowl is not big enough you could put the marinade and wings into a large freezer bag and shake until covered.)
- Preheat the halogen oven using the preheat setting or set the temperature to 210°C.
- Tip the wings and the coating onto the browning tray (or a baking tray or ovenproof dish if you don't have the browning tray). Cook on the low rack for 20 minutes or until the chicken is cooked.
- Serve with rice and salad.

# Moussaka

Using low fat crème fraîche instead of a white sauce is not only quicker but can save some calories.

- Place the aubergines in a pan of boiling water for 2 minutes. Remove and pat dry. Leave to one side.
- Meanwhile, heat a little olive oil in a sauté pan and fry the onion and garlic. Add the lamb mince and cook until brown.
- Add the tomatoes, tomato purée, mint, cinnamon and seasoning and cook for another 2–3 minutes.
- Select your ovenproof dish – I normally use a Pyrex or lasagne dish for this. Make sure it fits into your halogen cooker. Preheat your halogen using the preheat setting or set the temperature to 210°C.
- Place a layer of mince in the ovenproof dish, followed by a layer of aubergine. Continue alternating mince and aubergine, finishing with a layer of mince.
- Mix the crème fraîche with the grated cheese and pour it over the final layer of mince. Garnish with a sprinkle of grated cheese.
- Place on the low rack and cook for 20–25 minutes until bubbling.

**SERVES 4**

2–3 aubergines, sliced
Olive oil
1 onion
2 cloves of garlic, crushed
400g lamb mince
1 tin chopped tomatoes
2 teaspoons tomato purée
1 teaspoon dried mint
2 teaspoons cinnamon powder
Seasoning to taste
300ml low fat crème fraîche
50g mature cheddar or parmesan cheese, grated

# Toad in the Hole

100g plain flour
300ml milk
1 egg
1 onion, chopped
8 lean sausages
Olive oil
Handful of fresh herbs
   (e.g. thyme,
   oregano, rosemary)
   or 2 teaspoons dried
   herbs
Seasoning to taste

There is no reason why your halogen can't create your traditional family favourites.

- Preheat your halogen oven using the preheat setting or turn on to 200°C.
- Using a blender with a balloon whisk, blend the flour, milk and egg together to form a batter. Mix thoroughly and leave to settle.
- Meanwhile, place the onion, sausages and a drizzle of olive oil in a deep ovenproof dish that fits well inside your halogen oven. Place it on the high rack and cook for 8–10 minutes, turning occasionally.
- Just before the 10 minutes is up, give the batter mix a quick whizz with your balloon whisk, adding the herbs and seasoning before a final whizz.
- Remove the sausages from the oven and immediately pour over the batter, ensuring that all the sausages are covered.
- Return to the oven and cook on the low rack for 30–35 minutes until golden.
- Serve with onion gravy and steamed vegetables.

# Ham and Leek Cheesy Bake

Ham and cheese work so well together. This recipe just goes to prove that point!

- Cut the leeks to about 10–12.5cm (4–5in) in length and steam for 5–8 minutes until tender.
- Meanwhile, melt the butter gently in a saucepan on medium heat (not high!). Add the flour or cornflour and stir well with a wooden spoon. Add the milk, a little at a time, continuing to stir to avoid lumps.
- Switch to a balloon whisk and continue to stir over a medium heat until the sauce begins to thicken. The balloon whisk will help eradicate any lumps that may have materialised. Add more milk as necessary to get the desired thickness – the sauce should have the consistency of custard.
- If you are using nutritional yeast flakes, add these first as they will reduce the amount of cheese you may need – taste as you go! Then add the cheese and mustard, and stir well. Season with black pepper.
- Remove the leeks from the steamer and wrap a slice of ham or bacon around each one. Lay them in the base of an ovenproof dish – a lasagne dish is good for this but make sure it fits well inside your halogen oven.
- Preheat your halogen by using the preheat setting or set to 220°C.
- Pour the cheese sauce over the wrapped leeks. Combine the breadcrumbs, oats and parmesan cheese and sprinkle over the leeks.
- Place on the low rack and cook for 15 minutes until golden and bubbling.

4 leeks, trimmed top and tail
25g butter
1 tablespoon plain flour or cornflour
500–750ml milk
2 tablespoons nutritional yeast flakes (optional)
75g mature cheese
½ teaspoon mustard
Black pepper to taste
8 slices of lean ham or bacon
2–3 tablespoons home-prepared wholemeal breadcrumbs
2 tablespoons oats
25g parmesan cheese

# Traditional Cornish Pasties

SERVES 4–6

As I live on the Cornish border, it seems appropriate to include a traditional Cornish staple.

150g plain flour
75g cold butter
5–6 tablespoons cold
   water
1 onion
1 carrot
1 potato
100g swede
350g lean rump steak
1 teaspoon paprika
1 teaspoon mixed
   herbs (optional)
Seasoning to taste

- Make the pastry by placing the flour in a large bowl and adding small pieces of the chilled butter. Using your fingertips, rub the butter into the flour until the whole mix resembles breadcrumbs. Add the water (a little at a time) and mix until a dough is formed. Wrap the dough in cling film and place in the fridge to cool until needed.
- Chop the vegetables and steak into small dice-sized pieces. Place in a bowl and mix thoroughly. Add the paprika and herbs and season well.
- Roll out the pastry on a floured surface until even. Using a small, round plate (approximately 20cm in diameter) as a template, cut 4 circles.
- Preheat your halogen oven using the preheat setting or set the temperature to 210°C.
- Place some of the steak and vegetable mix in the centre of each pastry circle – do not overfill. Use beaten egg or water to brush the edges of the pastry before bringing the edges together and crimping until sealed.
- Place the pasties on a lined baking tray. Brush with beaten egg.
- Place on the lower rack of the oven and bake for 20 minutes until the pastry starts to turn golden. Reduce the heat to 150°C and cook for a further 20–25 minutes.

# Quiche Lorraine

SERVES 4–6

When making tarts, quiches or pies, I find it is much better to bake the pastry case first as this can prevent the horrible soggy bottom scenario. Personally I prefer using wholemeal or wholegrain flour to make a savoury pastry, but it is entirely your choice.

100g plain flour
50g cold butter
5–6 tablespoons cold water
200ml milk
3 eggs
½ teaspoon mustard powder
Pinch of cayenne pepper
150g Gruyère cheese, grated
1 small onion, finely chopped
75g cooked ham or lean bacon, diced
Seasoning to taste

- First make the pastry. Place the flour in a large bowl and add small pieces of the chilled butter. Using your fingertips, rub the butter into the flour until the whole mix resembles breadcrumbs. Add the water (a little at a time) and mix until a dough is formed. Wrap the dough in cling film and place in the fridge to cool until needed.
- Preheat the halogen oven using the preheat setting or set the temperature to 200°C.
- Roll out the pastry on a floured surface to the size and thickness needed to line a 23cm greased flan tin. Place a sheet of baking parchment over the pastry and cover with baking beans.
- Bake on the low rack in the halogen oven for 10 minutes. Remove the baking beans and parchment and cook for a further 5 minutes. Remove the pastry case from the oven and turn the temperature down to 190°C.
- Meanwhile, mix the milk and eggs together thoroughly before adding the mustard powder and cayenne pepper. Add the cheese, onion and bacon or ham. Season well before pouring into the pastry case.
- Bake on the low rack for 30–40 minutes until golden and the centre is firm. If the top starts to get too dark, cover with tin foil, making sure it is secure.

1 onion finely
    chopped
2–3 cloves of garlic,
    finely chopped
A spray of olive oil
1 pepper, finely
    chopped (optional)
400g lean beef mince
    or, for vegetarians,
    veggie mince
150ml red wine
75g mushrooms, finely
    chopped (optional)
3–4 fresh tomatoes,
    chopped, or 1 tin
    chopped tomatoes
Mixed herbs to taste
Seasoning to taste

# Lasagne

Everyone loves lasagne. You can speed up the cooking process by opting for fresh pasta sheets or you could boil the dried lasagne sheets for 8–10 minutes before adding to the dish. This will cut about 15 minutes off the cooking time.

- Fry the onion and garlic in a little olive oil until soft and translucent. Add the chopped pepper if you're including it.
- Add the mince and cook until brown, followed by the wine and mushrooms if you're using them. Cook for 2 more minutes.
- Add the tinned or fresh tomatoes (or 'cheat' pasta sauce), stirring well. Finally, add the herbs and season to taste. Leave to simmer for 5 minutes.
- While the Bolognese mixture is simmering, make the white sauce. Melt the butter gently in a saucepan on a medium heat (not high!). Add the flour or cornflour and stir well with a wooden spoon. Add the milk, a little at a time, continuing to stir to avoid lumps.
- Switch now to a balloon whisk. Continue to stir over a medium heat until the sauce begins to thicken. The balloon whisk will also help eradicate any lumps that may have formed. Add more milk as necessary to get the desired thickness. The sauce should have the consistency of custard. Add the mustard and season with black pepper.
- Preheat your halogen oven using the preheat setting or set the temperature to 210°C.
- Spoon a layer of Bolognese mix into the bottom of your lasagne dish (first make sure it fits into your

halogen), and then pour over a thin layer of white sauce, followed by a layer of lasagne sheets. (Remember that if you want to speed up the cooking process, you could boil the lasagne sheets for 8–10 minutes before adding or use fresh pasta sheets.) Continue alternating the layers, finishing with the white sauce. Don't overfill the dish as the lasagne may spill out during cooking.

- Sprinkle grated cheese over the top.
- Place on the low rack in the halogen oven and cook at 200°C for 40–50 minutes (or 30 minutes if using fresh or pre-boiled pasta sheets) until golden and the pasta sheets are cooked. If the top starts to get too dark, cover with tin foil, making sure it is secure.
- Serve with salad and garlic bread.

**For the white sauce:**
25g butter
1 tablespoon plain
  flour or cornflour
500–750ml milk
1/4 teaspoon mustard
  (optional)
Black pepper to taste

Sheets of lasagne
  (ensure the pack
  says 'no precooking
  required')
Grated cheese to
  garnish

800g potatoes, cut into
rough chunks
4 carrots, 2 roughly
chopped, 2 cut into
small cubes
A spray of olive oil
1 onion, chopped
400g lean mince (or
pre-drained of fat)
75g mushrooms, sliced
(optional)
100ml red wine
(optional)
200ml meat stock or
vegetable stock if
using veggie mince
1 teaspoon yeast
extract (Marmite or
similar)
Seasoning to taste
Worcestershire sauce
25g butter
75g mature cheddar
Paprika for sprinkling

# Shepherd's and Cottage Pie

The only real difference between shepherd's pie and cottage pie is the type of meat used. Shepherd's pie is traditionally made with lamb mince and cottage pie with beef. Nowadays you can make these dishes using a variety of minced meat, or vegetarian mince if you prefer.

- Steam the potatoes and the 2 chopped carrots until soft.
- Meanwhile, heat the oil in a large sauté pan and fry the onion for 1–2 minutes before adding the mince. Cook until brown and then add the 2 cubed carrots, the mushrooms and the wine.
- Heat the stock and then dissolve the yeast extract in it. Add this to the mince. Cook for 15 minutes until tender and reduced to the desired consistency. Season to taste and add the Worcestershire sauce.
- Preheat the halogen oven using the preheat setting or set the temperature to 200°C.
- Mash the steamed potato and carrots together. Add the butter and two thirds of the cheddar and mix thoroughly.
- Place the mince in a deep ovenproof dish and spoon the mash over the top. Be careful not to overfill the dish. Press the mash down gently with a fork. Top with the remaining grated cheese and a sprinkle of paprika.
- Place in the oven on the low rack and cook for 20–25 minutes.

# Chicken, Bean and Tomato One Pot

A very simple, wholesome and filling dish.

**SERVES 4**

- Preheat the halogen oven using the preheat setting or set the temperature to 200°C.
- In a roasting tin or casserole dish that fits inside your halogen, drizzle the oil and add the onion, pepper, garlic, chicken and tomatoes. Drizzle with a little more oil ensuring the ingredients are coated. Add the thyme and sprinkle with paprika.
- Place on the low rack and cook for 15 minutes.
- Remove from the oven and add all the remaining ingredients. Combine well.
- Place back in the oven and cook for another 20 minutes until the chicken is cooked to perfection.

Olive oil
2 red onions, cut into small wedges
1 red pepper, sliced
3–4 cloves of garlic, finely chopped
4 chicken breasts, halved
1 small punnet of cherry tomatoes, whole
Handful of fresh thyme (or 1–2 teaspoons dried)
2 teaspoons paprika
450ml chicken stock
2–3 teaspoons sundried tomato puree
1 tin cannellini beans, drained
Seasoning to taste
Small handful of fresh parsley, finely chopped

# Corned Beef and Potato Tart

SERVES 4

100g plain flour
50g cold butter
5–6 tablespoons cold
  water
3–4 potatoes, cooked
  and mashed (you
  can use leftover
  mash for this)
350g or 1 tin corned
  beef
1 onion, diced
1–2 teaspoons
  Worcestershire sauce
1 egg, beaten
Seasoning to taste

I prefer to bake the pastry case before adding the corned beef and potato mixture.

- Make the pastry: place the flour in a large bowl and add small pieces of the chilled butter. Using your fingertips, rub the butter into the flour until the whole mix resembles breadcrumbs. Add the water (a little at a time) and mix until a dough is formed. Wrap the dough in cling film and place in the fridge to cool until needed.
- Cook and mash the potatoes.
- Place the corned beef, mashed potato and diced onion in a bowl and mix thoroughly. Add the Worcestershire sauce and beaten egg and season well.
- Preheat the halogen oven using the preheat setting or set to 200°C.
- Roll out the pastry on a floured surface until even. Grease a pie dish, then line it with the pastry and trim to size. Bake blind by placing a piece of baking parchment over the pastry, adding the baking beans and cooking on the low rack for 10 minutes.
- Remove the baking beans and parchment and add the corned beef mix.
- Place back on the low rack and bake for 25 minutes.

# Pancetta and Gorgonzola Parcels

I love cabbage leaves stuffed with delicious flavours. Feel free to make your own variations to this tasty recipe.

8–12 large cabbage
  leaves
4 rashers of pancetta,
  chopped
1 small red onion,
  finely chopped
50–75g Gorgonzola,
  crumbled
Black pepper to taste
Water

- Place the cabbage leaves in a pan of boiling water for 2–3 minutes to soften the leaves. Remove and pat dry with kitchen paper or a clean tea towel.
- Place some of the pancetta, red onion and Gorgonzola in the centre of each leaf, season with black pepper and then roll into a parcel. If you need to, you can use a wooden cocktail stick to help secure the leaves in place.
- Place the cabbage parcel on a greased square of tin foil. Bring the sides of the foil up to form a well. Add 1 dessertspoon of water, and then secure the foil to form a parcel. Repeat this with all the cabbage parcels.
- When all the cabbage leaves are parcelled up, you can place them in and around other food, or place them together on the low rack of your halogen. Cook at 230°C for 15 minutes.
- Unwrap and serve.

Sausage meat
Puff pastry
Beaten egg
A sprinkle of sesame
  seeds (optional)

# Puffed Sausage Rolls

- Roll the sausage meat into a thumb-thick length.
- Roll out the pastry so that it is just over twice as wide as your roll of sausage meat, and 1cm longer at each end.
- Place the sausage mix 1–2cm from the long edge of the pastry.
- Coat the edges of the pastry with beaten egg before folding it over the sausage meat. Press down firmly on the edge before cutting the sausage rolls to the desired length.
- Preheat your halogen oven using the preheat settings or turn on to 210°C.
- Place the sausage rolls on a baking tray. Brush with beaten egg and sprinkle with sesame seeds before placing on the low rack and baking for 20–25 minutes until golden brown.

*Variations:* For a great variation to the standard sausage roll, mix some herbs with the sausage meat to create delicious Herby Sausage Rolls. If you like things hot, mix your sausage meat with some fresh chillies and a dollop of Tabasco sauce to create tempting Hot, Hot, Hot Sausage Rolls. Vegetarians can opt for any of the above by using vegetarian sausage mix.

# Spicy Meatballs in Rich Tomato Sauce

You can serve this with spaghetti for a lovely filling dish. Meatballs can be made in advance and frozen and the tomato sauce can also be cooked in advance and stored in a jar in the fridge or frozen.

- Combine all the meatball ingredients apart from the olive oil in a bowl and mix thoroughly.
- Form the mixture into small balls and place on a baking sheet. Cover the balls with a sheet of cling film and refrigerate for 30 minutes to rest.
- Preheat your halogen cooker using the preheat setting or set the temperature to 200°C.
- Place the meatballs in the bottom of an ovenproof dish, first making sure it fits in your halogen cooker. Drizzle with a little olive oil and place on the low rack for 15 minutes, rolling or turning halfway through.
- While that is cooking, combine the tomatoes, garlic, sugar, salt, drizzle of olive oil and chopped basil leaves.
- Remove from the oven and add the tomato sauce. Reduce the temperature to 180°C and place the meatballs in sauce back in the oven for another 15 minutes before serving with some spaghetti.

*Note:* You can freeze the meatballs raw. I normally place them, still on the baking tray, in the freezer until they are firm, before removing them from the tray and placing in a freezer bag. This way they won't stick together and you can pull out the required number of meatballs as and when you need them.

**Meatballs:**
400g beef mince
1 small onion, finely chopped or grated
1 teaspoon paprika
1 teaspoon cumin
1 chilli, finely chopped
1 teaspoon chilli powder
2 teaspoons Worcestershire sauce
1 teaspoon parsley
50g breadcrumbs
1 egg, beaten
Seasoning to taste
Drizzle of olive oil

**Tomato sauce:**
400g tin chopped tomatoes (or chopped fresh tomatoes)
2 cloves garlic, crushed
1 teaspoon sugar
½ teaspoon salt
Handful of chopped basil leaves
Drizzle of olive oil

# Bacon, Leek and Macaroni Cheese Bake

**SERVES 4**

175g macaroni
2–3 leeks, finely chopped
6–8 rashers of bacon, roughly chopped
Drizzle of olive oil
25g butter
1 tablespoon plain flour or cornflour
500–750ml milk
2 tablespoons nutritional yeast flakes (optional)
75g mature cheddar
½ teaspoon mustard
Black pepper to taste
2–3 tablespoons home-prepared wholemeal breadcrumbs
2 tablespoons oats
25g parmesan cheese

You can make this in advance and just pop it in the halogen when you are ready to heat it up, though make sure your sauce is not too thick when you add it to the mixture as it will thicken further when standing and again when cooking.

- Place the macaroni in boiling water and cook until tender. (The cooking time depends on the type of macaroni you use, so refer to the instructions on the packet.)
- While that is cooking, gently fry the leeks and bacon in a little olive oil or butter. Once cooked, leave to one side.
- Meanwhile, melt the butter gently in a saucepan on a medium heat (not high!). Add the flour or cornflour and stir well with a wooden spoon. Add the milk, a little at a time, continuing to stir to avoid lumps.
- Switch to a balloon whisk and continue to stir over a medium heat until the sauce begins to thicken. The balloon whisk will help to eradicate any lumps that may have materialised. Add more milk as necessary to get the desired thickness. The sauce should have the consistency of custard.
- If you are using nutritional yeast flakes, add these first as they will reduce the amount of cheddar you may need – taste as you go! Then add the cheese and mustard, and stir well. Season with black pepper.
- Drain the macaroni and combine it with the bacon, leek and cheese sauce. Season to taste and pour into an ovenproof dish, first making sure that it fits well in your halogen.

- Preheat your halogen oven by using the preheat setting or set at 220°C.
- Combine the breadcrumbs, oats and parmesan cheese and sprinkle over the bake.
- Place on the low rack and cook for 15 minutes until golden and bubbling.

# Beef Stroganoff

**SERVES 4**

You could opt to cook this on a hob in a sauté pan, but I have included this recipe to show you how versatile your halogen oven really is.

- Find a non-stick dish and place this on the high rack with a dash of olive oil. Set the temperature to 220°C.
- Place the beef, onion and garlic on the dish and cook for 3–6 minutes, turning occasionally.
- Add the mushrooms and butter and cook for another 3–6 minutes, until the mushrooms are tender but not too soft and the onion and beef are cooked.
- Add the herbs, sour cream and milk, and season to taste. Cover securely with tin foil. Place on the low rack and cook for another 8–10 minutes until the sauce is heated.
- Remove the tin foil, stir well and serve on a bed of pasta or rice.

Dash of olive oil
500g beef fillet or tenderloins, cut into very fine strips
2 onions, finely chopped
1–2 cloves of garlic, crushed
300g button mushrooms
15g butter
2 teaspoons chopped fresh tarragon (or 1 teaspoon of dried)
300ml sour cream
150ml milk
Seasoning to taste

# Mozzarella and Tomato Chicken

**SERVES 4**

4 chicken breasts
1 large ball of
 mozzarella, torn
2–3 ripe tomatoes,
 sliced
Handful of basil leaves
Seasoning to taste
4–6 slices of pancetta
 or Parma ham
Drizzle of olive oil

A very simple dish that takes minutes to prepare.

- Preheat the halogen oven using the preheat setting or set the temperature to 200°C.
- Using a sharp knife, cut a slit in each chicken breast to form a pocket. Stuff the pockets with the tomato slices, crumbled mozzarella and a few basil leaves. Season to taste.
- Wrap securely with pancetta or Parma ham. Place the wrapped chicken breasts, seam-side down, on a greased ovenproof dish. Drizzle with olive oil and season to taste.
- Place on the low rack for 20–30 minutes, until the chicken is cooked.

# Sausage Casserole

My Aunty Mabel used to make us a similar dish on Bonfire night when we stayed on the farm. This is a really hearty dish, perfect for autumn evenings.

- Preheat your halogen oven using the preheat setting or set the temperature to 230°C.
- Place the sausages, bacon and sliced onion on the browning tray. Drizzle with olive oil and cook on the high rack until the sausages are browned and the onion softened.
- In a casserole dish, first making sure it fits well in your halogen oven, add the sausages, onions and all remaining ingredients. Season to taste.
- Pop a lid on the casserole dish, or make a lid using double-folded tin foil, securely fastened.
- Place on the low rack and turn the temperature down to 200°C.
- Cook for 20–30 minutes until the vegetables are soft.
- Serve with mashed or jacket potatoes.

1 pack of lean, good quality sausages
4–6 rashers of bacon or lardons, chopped
1 large red onion, sliced
Drizzle of olive oil
2 cloves of garlic, crushed
2 red peppers, finely sliced
1 large sweet potato, diced
1 tin chopped tomatoes
175ml red wine
2 teaspoons paprika
Small handful of chopped parsley
Seasoning to taste

# Cheese, Bacon, Bread and Butter Savoury

**SERVES 4**

6 slices of stale bread, buttered
3–6 rashers of bacon, diced or roughly chopped depending on preference
1 onion, finely chopped
150g mature cheddar, grated
3 eggs
500ml milk
2 sprigs of thyme, chopped
Seasoning to taste

This is a variation of the lovely and comforting bread and butter pudding.

- Grease an ovenproof dish, first making sure it fits well in your halogen oven.
- Use some of the buttered bread to carefully line the dish. Add the bacon, onion and cheese between layers of bread, building up the layers until you run out of bread. Alternatively, you could make bacon, onion and cheese sandwiches and line the dish with them, but I prefer the randomness of the first method.
- Beat the eggs, add the milk and thyme and season to taste. Pour this over the bread and leave it to settle for about 20 minutes.
- Preheat your halogen oven using the preheat setting or turn to 180°C.
- Top the bread with some grated cheese and season with black pepper. Place on the low rack and cook for 30–40 minutes, until set.

# Roasted Herby Vegetables and Chicken Breasts

Another way to make a tasty chicken and vegetable dish.

- Preheat the halogen oven using the preheat setting or set the temperature to 200°C.
- In a large bowl, place the potatoes, sweet potato and parsnip. Add paprika and olive oil and combine until well coated.
- Pour this into an ovenproof dish. Add more oil if necessary. Cook for 15 minutes.
- Finely chop the herbs (you can use a mini electric chopper for this), retaining a small amount for the next step. Add the crushed garlic, 1–2 tablespoons of olive oil and the zest of 1 lemon. Combine well.
- Rub half of this mixture over the chicken breasts. Add the chicken to the potatoes and cook for another 15 minutes, before adding all remaining ingredients. Sprinkle the remaining herbs over the whole dish and combine well. Add more oil if necessary.
- Bake for another 20–30 minutes until the vegetables and chicken are cooked.

**SERVES 4**

600g small new
  potatoes, washed
1 large sweet potato,
  cubed
1 parsnip, quartered
  lengthways
2 teaspoons paprika
Olive oil
Large handful of fresh
  mixed herbs (such
  as thyme, rosemary,
  oregano)
3–4 cloves of garlic,
  crushed
Zest of 1 lemon
1 red onion, quartered
2–3 baby leeks, cut
  into 3 pieces
4–6 chicken breasts
1–2 red peppers,
  thickly sliced
8–12 small vine
  tomatoes, whole

SERVES 4

5 eggs

1 bunch of spring
onions, finely
chopped

1–2 red peppers, diced
or thinly sliced

6 rashers of pancetta,
diced

3–4 sundried
tomatoes, chopped

50g parmesan, grated

Small handful of fresh
herbs (basil, oregano
or thyme would suit
this dish)

Seasoning to taste

# Mediterranean-style Tortilla

This is an ideal dish for using up any leftover vegetables –
anything goes so experiment!

- Preheat the halogen oven using your preheat setting
  or set the temperature to 200°C.
- Beat the eggs well in a large bowl. Add all remaining
  ingredients and combine.
- Pour into a well-greased ovenproof dish. Place on the
  low rack and cook for 20–25 minutes until firm.
- Serve hot or cold with salad.

# Chicken and Bacon Parcels

SERVES 4

You can prepare these in advance as they do improve with a little marinating. Simple make them in the foil parcels and leave in the fridge until needed – ideally, prepare them the night before or in the morning before you leave for work.

- Preheat the halogen oven using the preheat setting or set the temperature to 200°C.
- Cut four double-thickness foil squares, large enough to hold the chicken breasts. Grease the middle of each square with oil or butter.
- In a mini chopper or by hand, mix the herbs, garlic, olive oil and lemon zest together.
- Place a few onion slices on each greased foil parcel.
- Using a teaspoon, smear the herb mixture on the chicken breasts to coat them. Add mushroom slices and wrap some bacon around each chicken breast. Place the breasts on top of the onion slices in each foil square.
- Add the tablespoon of white wine to each parcel before securing.
- Place the parcels on the low rack and cook for 35–40 minutes until the chicken is tender.
- Serve with new potatoes and green vegetables.

4 chicken breasts
Small handful of fresh thyme (or 1–2 teaspoons of dried)
2–3 cloves of garlic, crushed
1–2 tablespoons olive oil
Zest of 1 lemon
1 small red onion, finely sliced
6 mushrooms, sliced
4–6 rashers of bacon
4 tablespoons white wine
Seasoning to taste

SERVES 4

4–5 small potatoes,
cooked and mashed
(or you can use
leftover mash)
300g corned beef,
mashed
1 onion, finely
chopped
2 cloves of garlic,
crushed (optional)
1–2 teaspoons
wholegrain mustard
2–3 teaspoons tomato
puree
50g wholemeal
breadcrumbs
1 egg, beaten
Seasoning to taste

# Corned Beef Loaf

An easy dish that can be prepared in advance. Serve it hot or cold.

- Preheat your halogen oven using the preheat setting or set the temperature to 190°C.
- In a very large bowl put the mashed potato and mashed corned beef. Add all the remaining ingredients and combine well.
- Pour this into a lined loaf tin, pressing down firmly and smoothing out the top.
- Place on the low rack of the halogen oven and bake for 25 minutes.
- Leave to cool for 5 minutes before turning out onto a serving dish. The loaf can be served hot or cold, in slices.

# Hot Stuffed Chicken with Parma Ham

A simple dish that packs a punch. Enjoy with new potatoes and green vegetables.

- In a bowl, mix the cream cheese, lemon zest, chilli, garlic and chopped tomato together. Add the cayenne pepper and Tabasco sauce before seasoning to taste.
- Preheat your halogen oven using the preheat setting or set the temperature to 210°C.
- Using a sharp knife, cut a slit in each chicken breast to form a pocket. Use the cream cheese mixture to stuff each chicken breast. Then securely wrap Parma ham around the breast and place it, seal-side down, in an ovenproof dish.
- Drizzle with a little lemon juice and olive oil, and season to taste.
- Place on the low rack and cook for 25–30 minutes until the chicken is cooked.
- Serve with new potatoes and green vegetables.

1 tub of cream cheese
Zest and juice of 1 lemon
1 chilli, finely chopped
2 cloves of garlic, chopped
1 large tomato, finely chopped
1 pinch of cayenne pepper to taste
Dash of Tabasco sauce (optional)
Seasoning to taste
4 chicken breasts
4–6 slices of Parma ham
Olive oil

**SERVES 4**

Drizzle of olive oil
10–12 shallots, whole
(or small red onions,
quartered)
2 cloves of garlic,
crushed
250g button
mushrooms
2 carrots, diced
2 sticks of celery, finely
sliced
400g chicken breast or
thigh pieces
1 pack of lean bacon
or lardons, chopped
1 tin chopped
tomatoes
200ml red wine
1 bay leaf
Handful of chopped
parsley
2–3 sprigs of fresh
thyme
Seasoning to taste

# Coq au Vin

A hearty traditional dish, wonderful for an autumn or winter's evening.

- Preheat the halogen oven using the preheat setting or set the temperature to 210°C.
- In an ovenproof casserole dish, put the oil, shallots and garlic. Place in the halogen oven on the low rack and cook until the onion starts to soften.
- Add the mushrooms, carrots, celery and chicken pieces and cook for another 5 minutes. Then add all remaining ingredients. Combine well and season to taste.
- Cover with a lid or double-wrapped tin foil, securely fastened.
- Place back on the low rack and cook for 40–50 minutes until the vegetables and chicken are cooked to taste.

# Sausage in a Blanket

This is a traditional favourite for Christmas dinner to accompany the turkey, but why wait till Christmas?

- Preheat the halogen oven using the preheat setting or set the temperature to 200°C.
- Wrap bacon around each sausage and 1 sprig of rosemary. Place on a greased or non-stick baking tray, seam-side down.
- Drizzle with a little olive oil and place on the low rack and bake for 15–20 minutes until cooked.
- Serve with buttery mash, green vegetables and onion gravy.

**SERVES 4–6**

6–8 good quality sausages
8–10 rashers of lean bacon
2–3 sprigs of fresh rosemary
Drizzle of olive oil

# Stuffed Aubergine Bolognaise

2 aubergines
A spray of olive oil
1 onion, finely
   chopped
2–3 cloves garlic, finely
   chopped
1 pepper, finely
   chopped (optional)
400g lean minced
   meat or, for
   vegetarians, veggie
   mince
100ml red wine
75g mushrooms, finely
   chopped (optional)
3–4 fresh tomatoes,
   chopped, or 1 tin
   chopped tomatoes
Mixed herbs to taste
Seasoning to taste
Grated cheese to
   garnish

Double-up the recipe when you are making bolognaise and you can add it later to jacket potatoes, lasagne or this simple recipe.

- Preheat the halogen oven using the preheat setting or set the temperature to 180°C.
- Cut the aubergines in half lengthways. Using a sharp knife, criss-cross the middle of the aubergine, then scoop out the flesh in chunks. This can be used within the bolognaise sauce.
- Brush or spray a small amount of olive oil in the aubergine shell. Place the halves on a baking tray. If you have some leftover bolognaise, you can skip the next few steps. If not, continue as follows.
- In a sauté pan, fry the onion and garlic in a little olive oil until soft and translucent. Add the pepper if you are using one.
- Add the mince and cook until brown, followed by the wine and mushrooms if you are including them. Cook for 2 more minutes.
- Add the tinned or fresh tomatoes (or 'cheat' pasta sauce), stirring well. Finally, add the herbs and season to taste. Simmer for 5 minutes.
- Spoon the bolognaise mix into the aubergine halves, ensuring they are well covered.
- Sprinkle on grated cheese and season to taste.
- Place on the low rack in the halogen oven and cook for 30 minutes until the aubergines are soft.
- Serve with salad.

# Lamb Shanks

This recipe is a slow cook, enabling the lamb to become perfectly tender. You can speed things up if you want to, but you do risk a tougher lamb shank.

- Place the lamb shanks in a large freezer bag.
- In a bowl, combine the garlic, tomato puree, orange zest and juice, red wine, balsamic vinegar, rosemary, thyme and paprika. Season to taste.
- Pour this mixture into the freezer bag with the lamb shanks. Shake well to ensure the lamb is completely covered. Leave in the fridge overnight to marinate.
- When ready to cook, preheat the halogen oven using the preheat setting or set the temperature to 160°C.
- Remove the lamb shanks from the freezer bag and place them on a baking or roasting tray, first making sure the tray fits well in your halogen oven.
- Add all the remaining ingredients. Cover with a double layer of tin foil and secure well.
- Place this on the low rack and cook for 1 hour and 45 minutes – 2 hours. You could add some mini jacket potatoes (choose a recipe from Chapter 3) during the cooking time to accompany the dish.
- Remove the foil and cook for another 20–30 minutes until the lamb is tender and the sauce has thickened.

4 lamb shanks
3 cloves of garlic, crushed
3 tablespoons sundried tomato puree
Zest and juice of 2 oranges
250ml red wine
3 teaspoons balsamic vinegar
2–3 sprigs fresh thyme
2–3 sprigs fresh rosemary
2 teaspoons paprika
Seasoning to taste
2 red onions, cut into small wedges
2 sticks of celery, finely sliced
1 leek, finely sliced
1 carrot, finely diced
1 pepper, sliced
1 tin chopped tomatoes
300ml lamb stock
1 bay leaf

# Pea and Ham Soup

1 red onion, finely
chopped
1 desertspoon of olive
oil
25g butter
150g chopped cooked
ham
200g frozen peas
2 sticks of finely
chopped celery
400ml hot vegetable
stock
300ml milk
8 mint leaves
2 tablespoons creme
fraiche
Seasoning to taste

This is a bit of a cheat recipe but does work well.

- Preheat the halogen oven to 200°C.
- Remove the frozen peas from the freezer so they start to defrost at room temperature.
- Place the chopped onion, butter and olive oil in a small casserole dish and cook on the low rack for 8–10 minutes until the onion starts to soften. (The olive oil helps prevent the butter from burning). Make sure the casserole dish leaves plenty of room for the air to circulate.
- Add the ham and cook for another 3–5 minutes.
- Add the hot stock, milk, frozen peas, finely chopped celery, mint leaves and seasoning. Cover with a lid and cook for another 20–25 minutes.
- Carefully remove the casserole dish from the Halogen Oven. Add the creme fraiche and liquidise the soup using an electric hand/stick blender. Season to taste before servng.

# Cheat Chicken Tikka

SERVES 4

This is a really simple way to cook chicken tikka. I use Greek yoghurt as it holds better than natural yoghurt. Serve on a bed of rice with some extra sauce for dressing.

400g Greek yoghurt
½ onion, very finely chopped
2 cloves of garlic, finely chopped
1 chilli, finely chopped (optional)
3 tablespoons tikka paste
4 chicken breasts

- In a bowl, thoroughly combine the yoghurt, onion, garlic and tikka paste. Add the chilli if you like it hot.
- Add the chicken breasts to the bowl and cover them well with the tikka sauce. Cover the bowl with cling film and place it in the fridge to marinate overnight or for at least 1 hour.
- When you are ready to cook, turn the halogen oven to high as you are going to grill the chicken.
- Place the chicken on the grill pan or browning tray and grill for 8–10 minutes on each side, adding more sauce if and when needed.
- Serve on a bed of rice. Reheat any leftover sauce and pour it over the chicken prior to serving.

# Italian Beef Casserole

1 tablespoon plain
   flour
3 teaspoons paprika
500g lean beef steak,
   cut into chunks
Drizzle of olive oil
2 red onions, cut into
   wedges
2-3 cloves of garlic,
   finely chopped
2 red peppers, thickly
   sliced
200g pancetta, diced
300g cherry tomatoes
1 aubergine, diced
300ml red wine
300ml beef stock
2 tablespoons
   sundried tomato
   paste
Small handful of fresh
   thyme and oregano
   combined
100g olives
Seasoning to taste

A very filling dish that is surprisingly simple to prepare.

- Preheat the halogen oven using the preheat setting or set the temperature to 220°C.
- Place the flour and paprika in a bowl. Add the beef chunks and ensure they are evenly coated with the flour.
- Drizzle a little oil into a roasting tin and pop it into the halogen oven to heat on the high rack. Once heated, add the beef, onion and garlic. Return it to the halogen and cook for 5-10 minutes until browned and softened. You may need to stir it a few times during cooking to ensure the meat browns evenly.
- Remove the roasting tin from the oven and add the peppers, pancetta and cherry tomatoes. Cook again for another 5-8 minutes, stirring occasionally.
- Remove again and add all the remaining ingredients but only half of the fresh herbs. Combine well and season to taste. Cover with a double layer of tin foil, making sure it is securely placed.
- Place the dish on the low rack and turn the heat down to 160°C. Cook for 1 hour. Remove the tin foil and add the remaining herbs. Cook again without the tin foil lid for another 10 minutes.
- Serve with jacket potatoes.

# Ham, Sausage and Mushroom Ribbons

A tasty pasta dish – you can use spaghetti, tagliatelle or capellini.

- Preheat the halogen oven using the preheat setting or set the temperature to 210°C.
- Prepare the onion, garlic and sausages whilst the oven is heating up. Once the oven is at temperature, place them in an ovenproof dish with the olive oil and butter.
- Place this dish on the low rack and cook until the sausage slices start to brown and the onions start to soften. You will need to stir or turn them occasionally.
- Meanwhile, place the pasta in a pan of boiling water and cook according to the instructions on the packet.
- Add the button mushrooms to the dish and cook until they start to soften.
- While that is cooking, combine the milk, yoghurt and wholegrain mustard. Season to taste and add half the parsley.
- When the mushrooms and pasta are cooked, drain the pasta and add all the ingredients to the ovenproof dish, including the chopped ham. Place it back in the oven for 5–10 minutes just to heat through.
- Serve with the remaining parsley to garnish.

**SERVES 4**

1 onion, finely chopped
2 cloves of garlic
3–4 sausages, sliced
Drizzle of olive oil
10g butter
300g spaghetti, tagliatelle or angel hair (capellini) pasta
350g button mushrooms
150ml milk
150g Greek yoghurt
1–2 teaspoons wholegrain mustard
Seasoning to taste
1 small handful chopped parsley
100g thick ham, cut into chunks

# Turkey Lasagne

Why stick to red meat in your lasagne – turkey mince is tasty and very versatile.

**For the bolognaise:**

1 onion, finely
    chopped
2–3 cloves garlic, finely
    chopped
A spray of olive oil
1 pepper, finely
    chopped (optional)
400g turkey mince
150ml red wine
75g mushrooms, finely
    chopped (optional)
3–4 fresh tomatoes,
    chopped, or 1 tin
    chopped tomatoes
Mixed herbs to taste
Seasoning to taste

- Fry the onion and garlic in a little olive oil until soft and translucent. Add the pepper if you are including it.
- Add the mince and cook until brown, followed by the wine and mushrooms if you are using them, and cook for 2 more minutes.
- Add the tinned or fresh tomatoes (or 'cheat' pasta sauce), stirring well. Finally, add the herbs and season to taste. Leave to simmer for 5 minutes.
- While the bolognaise is simmering, make the white sauce. Melt the butter gently in a saucepan on a medium heat (not high!). Add the flour or cornflour and stir well with a wooden spoon. Add the milk, a little at a time, continuing to stir to avoid lumps.
- Switch now to a balloon whisk. Continue to stir over a medium heat until the sauce begins to thicken. The balloon whisk will help to eradicate any lumps that may have formed. Add more milk as necessary to get the desired thickness. The sauce should have the consistency of custard. Add the mustard and season with black pepper.
- Preheat the halogen oven using the preheat setting or set the temperature to 210°C.

- Spoon a layer of bolognaise mix into the bottom of your lasagne dish, first making sure it fits into your halogen oven, and then pour over a thin layer of white sauce, followed by a layer of lasagne sheets. Continue alternating the layers, finishing with the white sauce. Don't overfill the dish as the lasagne may spill out during cooking.
- Sprinkle grated cheese over the sauce.
- Place on the low rack in the halogen oven and cook at 200°C for 40–50 minutes until golden and the lasagne sheets are cooked. If the top starts to get too dark, cover it with tin foil, making sure it is secure. (The cooking time can be greatly reduced if you use fresh lasagne sheets.)
- Serve with salad and garlic bread.

**For the white sauce:**
25g butter
1 tablespoon plain
  flour or cornflour
500–750ml milk
¼ teaspoon mustard
  (optional)
Black pepper to taste

Sheets of lasagne
  (ensure the pack
  says 'no precooking
  required')
Grated cheese to
  garnish

4 pork chops or loin
   steaks
1 small tub of cream
   cheese
4–6 teaspoons of pesto
75g wholemeal
   breadcrumbs
30g parmesan cheese,
   grated
Seasoning to taste

# Pesto Pork

Perfect for the halogen oven – quick, simple and it tastes great.
Serve with a selection of roasted vegetables.

- Preheat the halogen oven using the preheat setting or
  set the temperature to 230°C.
- Place the chops or steaks on the grill tray and put it
  on the high rack. Grill for 3–4 minutes each side until
  they are almost cooked. Remove and put to one side.
- Mix the cream cheese and the pesto together
  thoroughly.
- In another bowl, mix the breadcrumbs and parmesan
  together and season to taste.
- Pour the pesto mix onto the pork, ensuring the tops
  are covered. Sprinkle on the breadcrumb mixture to
  finish.
- Place the tray back in the halogen on the high rack
  and cook until the topping is golden and bubbling.
  This should take no more than 5 minutes.

# Sausage and Mash Pie

This recipe turns a classic dish into a lovely one-pot.
Vegetarians can opt for veggie sausages instead of meat.

- Preheat the halogen oven using the preheat setting or set the temperature to 210°C.
- Place the potato, carrot and sweet potato in a steamer and cook until soft and ready to mash.
- Meanwhile, pour a drizzle of oil in the bottom of an ovenproof dish. Add the sausages, onion, garlic and redcurrant jelly. Combine well, ensuring the jelly is mixed.
- Place on the low rack and cook for 20 minutes. Stir with a wooden spoon a couple of times during cooking to combine the flavours again.
- When the sausages have cooked and browned, cut them into generous bite-size chunks. Add the wine and stock or gravy. Combine well. Place back in the oven and cook for another 10 minutes.
- If you need to thicken, mix the cornflour with a little water and pour onto the gravy, ensuring it is well combined.
- Mash the potato and vegetables, adding a little butter or milk.
- Remove the sausage mixture from the oven and place the mash on the top. Then place it back in the oven to brown for 10 minutes.
- Serve with green vegetables.

**SERVES 4**

4–5 potatoes, diced
2 carrots, diced
1 sweet potato, diced
Drizzle of olive oil
6–8 good quality sausages
1–2 red onions, sliced
1 clove of garlic, crushed
1 tablespoon redcurrant jelly
100ml red wine
200–300ml gravy or hot stock
1 teaspoon cornflour (optional)
25g butter or 75ml milk
Seasoning to taste

# Bubble and Squeak Patties

A great dish for using up any leftovers.

**SERVES 4–6**

500g leftover mashed
  or roast potatoes
400g leftover greens
½ bunch spring
  onions, finely
  chopped
100g feta cheese
1 teaspoon wholegrain
  mustard
Seasoning to taste
6–8 slices of bacon or
  pancetta

- Place your leftover potatoes and greens in a bowl. Add the spring onions, feta cheese and wholegrain mustard and mash or combine together thoroughly. This is much easier with mashed potato but, if you have leftover roasts, you could heat them slightly before mashing as it helps make them more pliable. Season to taste.
- Form into small patties, finishing with a wrap of bacon or pancetta. Place on a halogen grill or baking pan.
- Turn the halogen oven to high. Cook on the high rack, for 5–6 minutes on each side until golden and the bacon is cooked.
- Serve as a side dish with leftover roast meat.

# Feta, Pancetta and Onion Puff

SERVES 4

This is a light dish with a consistency similar to a soufflé. It makes a nice one-pot, supper-time dish.

- Put the breadcrumbs in a bowl. Place the milk, onion and bay leaf in a pan and bring to the boil.
- Remove the onion and bay leaf, leaving the onion to one side, and stir in the mustard. Pour this over the breadcrumbs and leave to stand for 20–30 minutes.
- When you are ready, preheat the halogen oven using the preheat setting or set the temperature to 200°C.
- Separate the eggs. Mix the egg yolk and all other ingredients, apart from the egg white, together with the soaked breadcrumbs. Chop the onion finely and add it to the mixture.
- Beat the egg whites until light and fluffy. Fold into the mixture carefully.
- Pour the mixture into a well-greased ovenproof dish. Bake on the low rack for 30–35 minutes.

100g fresh
  breadcrumbs
550ml milk
1 onion, halved or
  quartered
1 bay leaf
1 teaspoon wholegrain
  mustard
4 eggs
150g pancetta,
  chopped
100g feta cheese,
  crumbled
1 teaspoon dried
  thyme or small
  handful fresh
  chopped thyme
Seasoning to taste

# Fish

As a nutritionist, I strongly recommend you eat fish, preferably oily, omega-rich fish, at least two or three times a week. If you can, buy fresh. Here are some ideas to help inspire you. Some people say that you should never mix cheese and fish together but I disagree, so you will find some recipes including both these ingredients in this chapter.

# One-pot Roasted Fish, Fennel and Red Onion

2–4 white fish fillets
2 lemons
1 large or 2 small
  bulbs of fennel,
  sliced
2 red onions, sliced
2–3 cloves of garlic,
  finely sliced
Drizzle of olive oil
25g butter
Seasoning to taste

- Preheat the halogen oven using the preheat setting or set the temperature to 220°C.
- Prepare the fish fillets, season well and squeeze a little lemon juice over them. Leave the fish to one side until needed.
- Place the sliced fennel, onion, garlic and 1 lemon, cut into wedges, in a roasting or baking tray, first making sure the tray fits in your halogen oven.
- Drizzle with olive oil and place in the oven on the low rack for 15 minutes.
- Place the fish fillets on top of the vegetables and place a small knob of butter on each fillet. Squeeze the juice of 1 lemon and drizzle over the dish. Season to taste.
- Cover securely with foil. Bake for another 15–20 minutes until the fish is thoroughly cooked and flakes easily off the fork.
- Remove the foil and serve with new potatoes and a fresh green salad.

# Fish Burgers

SERVES 4

You can prepare the fish burgers in advance or freeze them until needed.

- In a large bowl, thoroughly mix together the spring onions, fish fillets, tarragon and lemon juice. Season before adding the beaten egg. Mix thoroughly.
- Gradually add the breadcrumbs and flour until you have a firm but moist mixture.
- Form the mixture into balls – again, these should be firm but moist. Use the palm of your hand to flatten the balls into burger shapes.
- You can place the burgers in the fridge until you are ready to use them, or freeze them in layers (separate each layer with parchment to prevent them from sticking together).
- When you are ready to cook the burgers, brush them lightly with olive oil. Turn the halogen oven to 250°C. Place them on the high rack and cook for 4–5 minutes on each side until golden. (You are actually grilling them at this heat!)
- Serve with wholemeal baps and a salad garnish, or chunky chips and peas for a variation on fish and chips.

½ bunch of spring onions, finely chopped
200g haddock fillet, finely chopped
200g white fish fillet, finely chopped
1 teaspoon tarragon
Juice of ½ lemon
Seasoning to taste
1 egg, beaten
1 tablespoon home-prepared wholemeal breadcrumbs
1 tablespoon flour

**SERVES 4**

1kg potatoes
500g fish fillets (or ask
    your fishmonger for
    pieces of flaky white
    fish)
200g salmon pieces
    (optional)
100g prawns
    (optional)
250ml milk
25g butter
25g flour
1 teaspoon mustard
Seasoning to taste
A little grated cheese
    for topping

# Creamy Fish Pie

Such a family favourite and perfect for the halogen oven. You can prepare this pie in advance.

• Boil or steam the potatoes until tender. Once they are cooked, mash with a little butter and place to one side.
• Meanwhile, place the fish and milk in a pan and bring the milk to the boil. Reduce the heat and cook gently for 10 minutes or until the fish is cooked through.
• Drain the fish and reserve the liquid for making the sauce. Shred the fish and place it in a pie dish.
• To make a creamy sauce, melt the butter in a pan and add the flour. Stir in the reserved milk stock and heat gently until the sauce thickens. I normally use a whisk at this stage as it helps prevent any lumps from forming. Stir continuously. Add the mustard and season to taste.
• Pour the sauce over the fish.
• Preheat the halogen oven using the preheat setting or set the temperature to 200°C.
• Cover the fish with mashed potato and top with a small amount of grated cheese.
• Place in the halogen on the low rack. Bake for 20–25 minutes until golden on top.

# Salmon, Sweet Potato and Chilli Fish Cakes

These fishcakes are packed with goodness – omega-rich salmon and antioxidant -rich sweet potato.

- Combine the breadcrumbs and semolina together, season and leave to one side.
- In a bowl mix together the fish, cooked and mashed sweet potato, spring onions, chillies, cumin, lemon juice and coriander. Add a little beaten egg to bind if necessary. Season to taste.
- Form the mixture into cakes – if it's too wet, add a little plain flour. Once the cakes are formed, you can leave them to rest or continue with the coating.
- To coat the fish cakes, brush each cake with a little beaten egg and then dip it into the breadcrumb mixture. This is a little messy so be prepared! Place the cakes on greased baking parchment and chill in the fridge for 10 minutes.
- Preheat the halogen oven using the preheat setting or set the temperature to 250°C.
- Remove the fishcakes from the fridge and brush with a light coating of olive oil, taking care not to displace the breadcrumb topping.
- Place the fishcakes on the high rack, either on a baking tray or browning pan or you can place them directly on the rack.
- Cook for 5–6 minutes on each side, turning to ensure they are evenly cooked and browned. (You are actually grilling them at this heat!)
- Serve with a lovely salad and new potatoes.

SERVES 4

50g breadcrumbs
2 tablespoons semolina
300g fresh or tinned salmon
350g sweet potatoes, cooked and mashed
3 spring onions, finely chopped
2 chillies, finely chopped
1 teaspoon ground cumin
1 tablespoon lemon juice
Small handful of coriander leaves, finely chopped
2 eggs, beaten
Olive oil

# Italian Fish Grills

SERVES 4

4 fish fillets (cod or
  coley)
Drizzle of lemon juice
4–6 rashers of
  pancetta
1 ball of mozzarella
4–8 sundried tomatoes
Small handful of fresh
  basil leaves
Seasoning to taste
Drizzle of olive oil

- Turn the halogen oven to high (to grill).
- Place the fish fillets on a grill tray and drizzle with a little lemon juice and olive oil. Grill for 2 minutes on the high rack.
- Turn the fillets over and add the pancetta to the grill tray beside (not on top) of the fish fillets. Grill for another 2 minutes, then remove from the oven.
- Layer pancetta, mozzarella, basil leaves and sundried tomatoes on the fish fillets. Season to taste and drizzle with a little olive oil.
- Place back in the halogen for another 3–4 minutes.

# Simple Baked Trout

- Preheat the halogen oven using the preheat setting or set the temperature to 200°C.
- Mix the butter and herbs together in a bowl to form a herb butter.
- Cut a piece of foil to almost double the size of the trout and butter it with the herb butter. Place the trout on the foil and drizzle lemon juice over it.
- Where the trout has been filleted, stuff with herb butter and a slice or two of lemon. Add the water. Drizzle with a dash of olive oil and season with black pepper.
- Seal the foil securely and place on a baking tray or directly on the low rack. Cook for 20–30 minutes until the fish is tender and flaking.
- Serve with new potatoes and green vegetables.

1–2 tablespoons butter
Small handful of fresh herbs (rosemary, sweet marjoram or dill, or a combination), finely chopped
Whole trout
1 lemon, sliced
1–2 dessertspoons water
Drizzle of olive oil
Black pepper to season

**SERVES 4**

400g haddock fillets,
  roughly chopped
2–3 hard-boiled eggs,
  halved or quartered
200ml crème fraîche
150ml milk
125g Gruyere cheese,
  grated
2 teaspoons
  wholegrain mustard
Seasoning to taste
2 tablespoons
  breadcrumbs
1 tablespoon oats
50g parmesan cheese,
  grated

# Haddock, Egg and Gruyere Bake

This is such a quick and easy dish and it's perfect for a comforting supper.

- Preheat the halogen oven using the preheat settings or turn on to 180°C.
- In an ovenproof dish, first making sure it fits in the oven, place the chopped haddock and hard-boiled eggs.
- In a bowl, mix the crème fraîche, milk, grated cheese and mustard. Season to taste. Spoon this over the egg and haddock mixture.
- Mix the breadcrumbs, oats and parmesan together. Season well and sprinkle over the crème fraîche mixture.
- Place on the low rack and bake in the oven for 15–20 minutes until the haddock is cooked.

# Tuna and Sweetcorn Lasagne

SERVES 4

Tuna and sweetcorn work so well together. If you want to speed up the cooking time, why not pre-boil the lasagne sheets for 8–10 minutes before adding. This can knock off 15 minutes from the cooking time. Alternatively you could opt for fresh pasta sheets but these are more expensive.

400g tuna (roughly 2 tins), mashed
3–4 spring onions, chopped
200g sweetcorn (tinned or frozen)
Seasoning to taste
Lasagne sheets
500ml passata
Grated parmesan or other cheese for topping

• Mix the tuna, spring onions and sweetcorn together in a bowl. Season to taste.
• Add a layer of this tuna mash to the bottom of a lasagne dish, cover with a layer of lasagne sheets (remember to pre-boil if you want to speed up the cooking process) and top with a layer of passata. Repeat this process, ending with a layer of passata.
• Preheat the halogen oven using the preheat setting or set the temperature to 210°C.
• Grate parmesan or other cheese over the top layer of passata and sprinkle with black pepper.
• Place on the low rack and cook for 40–50 minutes (30 minutes if you are using pre-boiled or fresh pasta sheets) until golden and the lasagne sheets are cooked. If the top starts to get too dark, cover with tin foil, making sure it is secure.
• Serve with salad and garlic bread.

# Baked Sea Bass with Red Pesto

**SERVES 4**

4 sea bass fillets
1 red onion, sliced
4 slices of lemon
Drizzle of olive oil
1–2 tablespoons white
  wine
Seasoning to taste
4 teaspoons of red
  pesto

- Preheat the halogen oven using the preheat setting or turn on to 200°C.
- Cut out four squares of tin foil, twice the size of each fillet. Grease each one with a little butter.
- Place one slice of lemon in the middle of each square. Place a fillet on top of it. Add 1 teaspoon of red pesto to each fillet. Cover with some onion slices.
- Drizzle with a dash of olive oil and a dash of white wine. Season well and secure the foil into a parcel.
- Place on the low rack and cook for 20–25 minutes until the fish is cooked and flaky.

# Tomato and Tuna Gratin

- Preheat the halogen oven using the preheat setting or set the temperature to 200°C.
- Chop the tuna into chunks and place in an ovenproof dish.
- Heat the olive oil in a sauté pan. Add the onion, garlic and red pepper and cook until they start to soften. Add the chopped tomatoes, balsamic vinegar and herbs. Season to taste. Pour this over the tuna.
- In a bowl, mix the breadcrumbs, oats and grated cheese and season to taste. Sprinkle this mixture over the tomato mixture.
- Place in the oven on the low rack and cook for 15 minutes.

400g tinned tuna
Drizzle of olive oil
1 red onion, finely chopped
2 cloves of garlic, crushed
½ red pepper, diced
1 tin chopped tomatoes
Dash of balsamic vinegar
Small handful of basil, chopped
½ teaspoon dried thyme
Seasoning to taste
75g breadcrumbs
50g oats
50g mature cheddar, grated

# Red Snapper and Tomato Bake

500g red snapper
fillets
Seasoning to taste
Drizzle of olive oil
2 cloves of garlic,
crushed
1 red onion, finely
chopped
50g sundried
tomatoes, chopped
3 ripe vine tomatoes
200ml red wine
Handful of fresh basil,
chopped

- Preheat the halogen oven using the preheat setting or turn the temperature to 190°C.
- Place the fish fillets in an ovenproof dish. Season to taste.
- In a sauté pan, add the oil, garlic and red onion. Fry until the onion starts to become translucent. (If you prefer, you can cook the onion and garlic in the halogen oven by placing on the high rack and cooking on high heat until translucent. Add this to the fish, and then add the remaining ingredients. Add the basil once you have removed the dish from the halogen.)
- Add the tomatoes, wine and most of the basil to the sauté pan. Cook for another 2–3 minutes. Remove and pour over the fish.
- Cover the ovenproof dish with foil. Bake on the low rack for 20 minutes until the fish is cooked.
- Garnish with the remaining basil to serve.

# Baked Plaice and Potatoes with Cherry Tomato and Basil Drizzle

**SERVES 4**

- Preheat the halogen oven using the preheat setting or set to 200°C.
- Place the new potatoes, paprika, mixed herbs and a drizzle of olive oil in a bowl. Combine well. Pour into a baking tray (first making sure it fits in the halogen oven) and place on the low rack for 25 minutes.
- In a small baking dish, combine the cherry tomatoes, garlic, half the basil and a drizzle of olive oil. Season with the sugar, a sprinkle of salt and some black pepper. Combine well, cover with foil and leave to rest until needed.
- Season the fish and drizzle with lemon juice. Place the fish over the almost cooked new potatoes.
- Place the tomato and basil mixture on the high rack above the fish and cook for 10–15 minutes until the fish and the potatoes are cooked.
- To serve, place baked potatoes and fish on the plate. Stir the remaining fresh basil into the tomato and basil mixture and drizzle it over the potatoes and fish. Serve with steamed green vegetables.

1kg new potatoes, washed
2 teaspoons paprika
1 teaspoon mixed dried herbs
Drizzle of olive oil
200g cherry tomatoes, halved
2–3 cloves of garlic, finely sliced
Small handful of fresh basil
1 teaspoon sugar
Seasoning to taste
4 small pieces of plaice, prepared and trimmed
Drizzle of lemon juice

# Baked Herbie Salmon

SERVES 4

Handful of fresh basil
Small handful of fresh
  dill
Juice of 2 lemons
30–40ml olive oil
1 red onion, sliced
1 whole salmon,
  boned, trimmed and
  ready to cook

- Preheat the halogen oven using the preheat setting or set the temperature to 200°C.
- Place the herbs, lemon juice and olive oil in a processor and whizz until combined.
- Cut a piece of tin foil large enough to parcel the salmon. Butter the foil and add the sliced onion. Place the salmon over the onion.
- Stuff the salmon with half of the herb paste and use the remaining paste to cover it.
- Fold the foil around the salmon to parcel it, making sure the edges are sealed well.
- Place on the low rack and cook for 25–35 minutes depending on the size of the fish and until it flakes easily.
- Unwrap and serve with new potatoes and green vegetables.

# Creamy Baked Haddock

- Preheat the halogen oven using the preheat setting or set the temperature to 180°C.
- Butter the base of an ovenproof dish, first making sure it fits in your halogen oven.
- Butter and season the fillets, then roughly chop them. Place them in the ovenproof dish combined with the sliced onion.
- In a bowl, mix the lemon zest and juice, mustard, crème fraîche, milk, parsley and season with black pepper. Combine well.
- Pour this over the fish and spread evenly. Sprinkle with grated parmesan and black pepper.
- Place on the low rack and cook for 25–30 minutes until the fish is tender.

800g haddock fillets
1 red onion, sliced
40g butter
Seasoning to taste
Juice and zest of 1 lemon
2 teaspoons wholegrain mustard
150ml crème fraîche
150ml milk
Small handful fresh parsley, chopped
Black pepper
Parmesan cheese, grated

# Salmon Honey and Mustard Crusts

4 salmon fillets
Juice of ½ lemon
1–2 tablespoons
   wholegrain mustard
1–2 tablespoons honey
2 tablespoons
   wholemeal
   breadcrumbs
1 tablespoon
   cornflakes, crushed
   (if you don't have
   cornflakes, use finely
   chopped nuts)

*Simple yet delicious.*

- Preheat the halogen oven using the preheat setting or set the temperature to 200°C.
- Squeeze some lemon juice over the salmon fillets.
- Mix the mustard and honey together. In another bowl, mix the breadcrumbs and cornflakes together.
- Spread the mustard and honey mixture onto the fillets, ensuring they are well coated. Then dip the fillets into the breadcrumbs, again ensuring they are well coated.
- Place the fillets on a baking tray and place on the low rack. Cook for 12–15 minutes until they are cooked.
- Serve with a green salad and new potatoes.

# Stuffed Trout

- Preheat the halogen oven using the preheat setting or set the temperature to 190°C.
- Place the trout in an ovenproof dish. Squeeze lemon juice over it and season.
- In a sauté pan, sauté the onion and bacon in a little olive oil. (You can do this in the halogen if you prefer on the high rack and using the high heat – remember to turn the temperature back down afterwards.) Once cooked, remove and place in a mixing bowl.
- Add the breadcrumbs, zest and remaining lemon juice, parsley and cream cheese. Mix together thoroughly, then use this mixture to stuff the trout.
- Cover with foil and place on the low rack of the halogen. Cook for 20 minutes or until the trout is flaking.
- Serve with new potatoes and green vegetables.

1 trout, filleted and prepared to stuff
Juice and zest of 1 lemon
Seasoning to taste
Drizzle of olive oil
1 small onion, finely chopped
3–4 rinds of bacon, chopped
75g breadcrumbs
Small handful of fresh parsley, chopped
200g cream cheese

# Tomato, Prawn and Fish Stew

Drizzle of olive oil

1 onion, finely chopped

2 cloves of garlic, crushed

1 red pepper, deseeded and diced

1 tin chopped tomatoes, or 6 ripe tomatoes

300ml warm fish stock

300ml white wine

520g fish fillets or pieces

12 prawns

2 bay leaves

Handful of fresh parsley, chopped

Seasoning to taste

- Heat the oil in a sauté pan and fry the onion, garlic and pepper for 2–3 minutes.
- Select a casserole or ovenproof dish, making sure it fits well in your halogen oven. Preheat the halogen using the preheat setting or set the temperature to 180°C.
- Place the onion mixture and all the remaining ingredients into the dish and combine well. Season to taste.
- Cover with a lid or piece of tin foil, secured well.
- Place on the low rack and cook for 40 minutes before serving.

# Red Mullet with Mushroom and Cashew Stuffing

SERVES 4

- Preheat the halogen oven using the preheat setting or set the temperature to 190°C.
- Place your prepared fish on squares of tin foil. Squeeze over lemon juice and season.
- In a sauté pan, sauté the onion in a little olive oil. Add the chopped mushrooms, cashew nuts, breadcrumbs and yeast extract. (I use a food processor to finely chop all these ingredients.) Cook for a couple of minutes before adding the parsley.
- Use this mixture to stuff each fillet.
- Add the water and ½ teaspoon of butter to each tin foil square. Season to taste before folding the foil around the fish.
- Place on the low rack of the halogen and cook for 20 minutes or until the fish is flaking.
- Serve with new potatoes and green vegetables.

4 small red mullet, filleted and prepared to stuff
Juice of 1 lemon
Seasoning to taste
Drizzle of olive oil
1 small onion, finely chopped
125g mushrooms, finely chopped
125g cashew nuts, finely chopped
40g breadcrumbs
1 heaped teaspoon yeast extract
Small handful of fresh parsley, chopped
4 dessertspoons water
2 teaspoons butter

# Salmon Fish Cakes

400g fresh or tinned
salmon

400g potatoes, cooked
and mashed

2 teaspoons lemon
juice

1–2 teaspoons fresh
dill (or 1 teaspoon
dried)

1–2 teaspoons fresh
tarragon (or 1
teaspoon dried)

2 eggs, beaten

Drizzle of olive oil

A little plain flour

- Mix the fish, potatoes, lemon juice and herbs together in a bowl. Add the egg to bind.
- Form the mixture into cakes. If they are too wet roll in a little plain flour, but dust off to remove any excess flour. Place the cakes on baking parchment and chill in the fridge for 10 minutes.
- Preheat the halogen oven using the preheat setting or set the temperature to 250°C.
- Remove the cakes from the fridge and brush them with a light coating of olive oil. Place them on the high rack, either on a baking tray or browning pan or directly on the rack.
- Cook the cakes for 5–6 minutes each side, ensuring that both sides are evenly cooked and browned. (You are actually grilling them at this heat!)

# Cod and Cheese Gratin

- Preheat the halogen oven using the preheat setting or set the temperature to 180°C.
- Mix the crème fraîche, parsley, mustard and mature cheese in a bowl. Season to taste.
- Place the fish pieces in the bottom of an ovenproof dish, first making sure it fits well in the halogen oven. Pour the crème fraîche mixture over the fish.
- Mix the oats, breadcrumbs and parmesan together. Season and sprinkle on top of the crème fraîche mixture.
- Place on the low rack and cook for 15–20 minutes.

250g tablespoons crème fraîche
Small handful of fresh parsley, chopped
1 teaspoon wholegrain mustard
100g mature cheese
Seasoning to taste
3–4 skinless cod fillets, roughly chopped
100g oats
100g breadcrumbs
50g parmesan, grated

# Italian-style Cod

SERVES 4

4 cod fillets
1–2 tablespoons pesto
1 red onion, sliced
   into rings
6–8 sprigs of fresh
   thyme
4 rashers of pancetta
Dash of olive oil
Black pepper

- Preheat the halogen oven using the preheat setting or set the temperature to 220°C.
- Cover each fillet with a layer of pesto and add some onion rings and fresh thyme. Wrap a rasher of pancetta around each fillet and place it on a square of greased baking parchment or foil, large enough to package the fillet securely. Drizzle with a dash of olive oil and season with black pepper.
- Seal the parcels and place them on a baking tray or directly on the low rack. Cook for 15–20 minutes until the fish is tender and flaking.
- Serve with new potatoes and green vegetables.

# Breaded Salmon Fillets

This is so simple but tastes divine and looks quite impressive. Serve with green salad and new potatoes.

- Preheat the halogen oven using the preheat setting or set the temperature to 220°C.
- Place the breadcrumbs, oats, chives, parsley, parmesan, lemon zest and juice in a bowl and combine well.
- Cover the fillets in cream cheese (or just the tops if you don't want to get too messy!).
- Dip the fillets into the breaded mixture, ensuring they are well covered, and then place them on a greased or lined baking tray.
- Place on the low rack and bake in the oven for 20 minutes.
- Serve with salad and new potatoes.

50g home-prepared
  breadcrumbs
1 tablespoon oats
1 tablespoon chives
1 tablespoon parsley
1 tablespoon grated
  parmesan cheese
Zest of 1 lemon
Juice of ½ lemon
4 salmon fillets (or any
  other fish fillet)
4–5 teaspoons low fat
  cream cheese

# Salmon and Herb Butter Parcels

**SERVES 4**

1–2 tablespoons butter
Small handful of fresh herbs (e.g. parsley and dill), finely chopped
4 salmon fillets
1 lemon, sliced
4 dessertspoons water
Dash of olive oil
Black pepper to season

- Preheat the halogen oven using the preheat setting or set the temperature to 220°C.
- Mix the butter and herbs together to form a herb butter.
- Cut 4 squares of foil, large enough to parcel each fillet.
- Cover each fillet with a layer of herb butter, a slice or two of lemon and 1 dessertspoon of water. Drizzle with a dash of olive oil and season with black pepper.
- Seal the parcels and place them on a baking tray or directly on the low rack. Cook for 15–20 minutes until the fish is tender and flaking.
- Serve with new potatoes and green vegetables.

# Simple Mackerel Parcels

SERVES 4

- Preheat the halogen oven using the preheat setting or set the temperature to 200°C.
- Prepare the fish and season well.
- Cut 4 squares of foil, large enough to parcel each fillet. Grease well.
- Place each fillet in the centre of the foil. To each fillet add 1 teaspoon of butter, 1 lemon slice and 1 dessertspoon of water. Season and wrap securely.
- Place the fish parcels on the low rack and cook for 20 minutes.
- Unwrap and serve immediately.

4 mackerel, filleted
40g butter
4 slices of lemon
4 dessertspoons of
   water
Seasoning to taste

# Haddock Florentine

180g spinach
500–700ml milk
400g haddock fillets
20g butter
20g plain flour
100g mature cheddar
1 teaspoon wholegrain
  mustard
Pinch of cayenne
  pepper
Seasoning to taste

- Preheat the halogen oven using the preheat setting or set the temperature to 210°C.
- Steam the spinach for 5 minutes so that it wilts. Once soft, place it in a greased ovenproof dish and push down to form a base.
- Bring the milk to the boil and add the haddock fillets. Cook gently until the haddock is cooked (flaking off the fork). Remove the fish and flake/chop onto the bed of spinach.
- Meanwhile, melt the butter in a saucepan. Add the flour to form a paste. Gradually add the hot milk and stir well. Use a balloon whisk to remove any lumps.
- Add almost all the cheese, retaining some for the topping. Add the mustard and cayenne pepper and season to taste. Once the cheese has melted, pour this sauce over the haddock mixture.
- Garnish with remaining cheese. Place on the low rack and cook for 10–15 minutes until golden on top.

# Salsa Chilli Red Mullet

- Preheat the halogen oven using the preheat setting or set the temperature to 190°C.
- Place the fish fillets in an ovenproof dish. Squeeze over lime juice and season.
- Chop and prepare the remaining ingredients. Mix together thoroughly and pour over the fish fillets.
- Cover with foil and place on the low rack of the halogen. Cook for 20 minutes or until the fish is flaking.
- Serve with new potatoes and green vegetables.

4 red mullet fillets
Juice of 1 lime
Seasoning to taste
1 tablespoon olive oil
3 ripe tomatoes, chopped
1 small red onion, diced
1 red pepper, diced
1–2 chillies, finely chopped
2–3 cloves of garlic, crushed
Small handful of coriander leafs, chopped
200ml vermouth

# Slow-baked Tomato and Tuna Bake

**SERVES 4**

Olive oil
2 cloves of garlic,
  crushed
1 red onion, finely
  chopped
4–6 ripe tomatoes,
  quartered
Sprinkle of sea salt
Sprinkle of sugar
1 dessertspoon
  balsamic vinegar
Handful of chopped
  fresh basil
300g dried pasta twirls
300g tuna, crumbled
50g mozzarella
Black pepper to
  season

- Preheat the halogen oven using the preheat setting or turn the temperature to 170°C.
- Place the oil, garlic, onion and tomatoes in an ovenproof dish. Sprinkle with sea salt, sugar and balsamic vinegar. Add half of the fresh basil.
- Place on the low rack and cook for 20–30 minutes. While this is cooking, cook and drain the pasta, following the instructions on the packet.
- Remove the tomatoes from the halogen once cooked. Add the cooked pasta and crumbled tuna. Combine well. Finish with crumbled mozzarella, a drizzle of olive oil and season with black pepper.
- Bake on the low rack for 10–15 minutes at 190°C then serve immediately.

# Smoked Mackerel and Leek Pie

*A variation to the family favourite.*

- Cut the potato and sweet potato into pieces of an equal size ready to steam.
- While the potatoes are steaming, fry the leeks in a little butter to soften them.
- Place the softened leeks in a bowl and add the mackerel, crème fraîche, Greek yoghurt, parmesan and parsley. Mix thoroughly and season to taste. If it looks too dry, add a little milk. Pour this mixture into an ovenproof pie dish.
- Mash the potatoes together with a little butter and season well. Place over the mackerel mixture.
- Place on the low rack and cook at 200°C for 20–25 minutes until golden.

600g potatoes
300g sweet potatoes
2–3 leeks, diced
40g butter
400g smoked mackerel fillets, diced
200ml crème fraîche
100ml Greek yoghurt
50g parmesan, grated
Small handful of freshly chopped parsley
Dash of milk (optional)
Seasoning to taste

# Salmon Fish Fingers

SERVES 4

30g plain flour
75g oatmeal
50g parmesan, grated
75g breadcrumbs
Seasoning to taste
1–2 eggs, beaten
2–4 salmon fillets

This is a really simple idea for the frozen fish fingers kids seem to adore. You can opt for any white fish instead of salmon if you prefer.

• Preheat the halogen oven using the preheat setting or set the temperature to 210°C.
• In a bowl, mix the flour, oatmeal, parmesan and breadcrumbs. Season to taste.
• In another bowl, beat the eggs.
• Cut the salmon into thick fingers. Dip them into the egg mixture and then into the breadcrumb mixture, ensuring at each stage that the fish is evenly coated.
• Place on a well-greased ovenproof tray. Cook on the low rack for 15–20 minutes until crunchy and the salmon is cooked.
• Serve with potato wedges (see Chapter 3 on potato recipes).

# Individual Haddock Puff Pies

SERVES 4–5

Cook these pies in small ramekin dishes. If you prefer to cook this as one large dish feel free, but you may need to adjust the cooking time.

- Preheat the halogen oven using the preheat setting or set the temperature to 210°C.
- In a bowl, mix the haddock pieces with the crème fraîche, milk, lemon zest, and season to taste. Combine well.
- Place this mixture in the ramekin dishes, leaving a little room to add the halved soft-boiled egg. Cover with grated cheese.
- Roll out the puff pastry to a 2–3mm thickness. Cut out pastry lids to cover the ramekin dishes. To seal the lids you may need to place a small amount of pastry around the edges of each dish to form a lip and to give something for the pastry to grip on to. Then seal with a little milk or water. Cut a small slit in the top of each pastry lid to allow the air to escape. Brush with milk, beaten egg or water.
- Place on the low rack and cook for 20 minutes.

450g haddock pieces
200ml crème fraîche
75ml milk
Zest of 1 lemon
Seasoning to taste
2–3 soft-boiled eggs, halved
30–50g mature cheese, grated
¼ of a pack of puff pastry

# Cheesy Pollack Layer

SERVES 4

4 pollack fillets
Juice and zest of 1
    lemon
100g baby leaf spinach
3 tomatoes, sliced
250g crème fraîche
200ml milk
100g parmesan cheese
40g breadcrumbs
40g oats
Seasoning to taste

A filling dish with multiple layers of flavour. If you don't want to use pollack, you can opt for cod or even coley.

- Preheat the halogen oven using the preheat setting or set the temperature to 200°C.
- Squeeze almost all of the lemon juice over the fillets and leave to one side.
- In the base of an ovenproof dish, place a layer of spinach leaves. On top of this, add the slices of tomato. Season with black pepper.
- Place the fish fillets over the tomatoes. Add the remaining lemon juice and the lemon zest.
- In a bowl, mix the crème fraîche, milk and 75g of grated parmesan cheese. Season to taste before pouring over the fish.
- In another bowl, mix the breadcrumbs, oats and remaining parmesan. Mix and season well. Sprinkle this over the sauce.
- Place in the oven on the low rack and cook for 25 minutes until golden.

# Grilled Wholegrain Cod

A simple dish with a crispy coating of wholegrain mustard.

SERVES 4

- Preheat the halogen oven using the preheat setting or set the temperature to 200°C.
- Squeeze some lemon juice over the fillets.
- Mix the mustard, breadcrumbs, oats and black pepper together.
- Brush the fillets with olive oil. Spread on the mustard coating, ensuring the tops of the fillets are well coated.
- Place the fillets on a baking tray and cook on the low rack for 12–15 minutes until the fish is cooked.
- Serve with a green salad and new potatoes.

4 cod fillets
Juice of 1 lemon
2–3 tablespoons
   wholegrain mustard
75g wholemeal
   breadcrumbs
50g oatmeal
Black pepper to taste
Drizzle of olive oil

3cm knuckle of ginger,
    finely chopped
2–3 chillies, finely
    chopped
1–2 sticks of
    lemongrass, finely
    chopped
Juice and zest of 1
    lime
3–4 lime leaves,
    chopped
4 teaspoons Thai paste
Tin of coconut milk
150ml Greek yoghurt
Seasoning to taste
Small handful of fresh
    coriander leaves,
    chopped
4 fish fillets
400g of Cooked Thai
    Lime Rice

# Thai Fish Bakes

You can use whatever fish you prefer in this recipe. Simply prepare the Thai sauce, pour it over the fish and secure in foil. For added flavour, why not marinate the fish for an hour or two before baking. You could opt to use a Thai meal kit, which contains coconut milk, Thai paste, herbs and spices and costs less than £2 – cheaper than buying each item individually.

- Prepare the Thai sauce by mixing together the ginger, chillies, lemongrass, lime, Thai paste, coconut milk and Greek yoghurt. Season to taste before adding half the coriander.
- Place each fish fillet on a double-layer tinfoil square, large enough for a portion of rice to be added later and to fold and secure into a parcel.
- Pour over the Thai sauce, dividing it evenly between each portion – if there is any sauce left over, leave it to one side for later. Leave to marinate for at least 1 hour.
- Preheat the halogen oven using the preheat setting or set the temperature to 180°C.
- Place the parcels on the low rack and cook for 15 minutes.
- Meanwhile, cook the Thai rice. Once cooked, undo each parcel. Add a portion of rice to each parcel with any remaining sauce and reseal. Place back in the oven and cook for a further 5–8 minutes.
- To serve, garnish with coriander leaves.

# Salmon, Ricotta and Cheese Cannelloni

This is such a simple dish to make, but it looks impressive and tastes even better!

- Place the spinach in a colander and run under hot water for a couple of minutes to soften the leaves.
- In a bowl, mix together the salmon, ricotta, baby leaf spinach, lemon zest, dill and nutmeg.
- Cook the dried lasagne sheets in boiling water for 5–8 minutes and then drain.
- Add the salmon and ricotta mixture to one end of each sheet. Roll up firmly to form cannelloni tubes and place seal-side down in an ovenproof dish in a single layer.
- Preheat the halogen oven using the preheat setting or set the temperature to 190°C.
- Whilst the oven is preheating, mix the crème fraîche, onion, cheese and seasoning together and pour this over the cannelloni.
- Sprinkle with a mixture of breadcrumbs and parmesan before placing on the low rack. Cook for 30 minutes, until the cannelloni is cooked.
- Serve with garlic bread and green salad.

**SERVES 4**

- 50g fresh baby leaf spinach
- 300g salmon fillets, shredded
- 1 tub of ricotta
- Zest of 1 lemon, finely chopped
- Small handful of fresh dill, finely chopped
- ¼ teaspoon grated nutmeg
- 8 lasagne sheets
- 500g crème fraîche
- 1 small red onion, finely chopped
- 75g mature cheddar
- Seasoning to taste
- 50g breadcrumbs
- 30g parmesan, grate

# Salmon, Garlic and White Wine Parcels

**SERVES 4**

3–4 cloves of garlic, crushed
1 tablespoon honey
1 tablespoon wholegrain mustard
1 tablespoon balsamic vinegar
2 tablespoons white wine
Zest of 1 lemon
1 small onion, sliced into onion rings
4 salmon fillets
Small handful of fresh dill, finely chopped
Seasoning to taste

This recipe takes only minutes to prepare and around 15 minutes to bake. Also, you can prepare the parcels in advance.

• Preheat the halogen oven using the preheat setting or set the temperature to 200°C.
• Place the garlic, honey, mustard, balsamic vinegar, white wine and lemon zest in a bowl and combine well.
• Cut 4 squares out of double-thickness tin foil, big enough to parcel the salmon fillets.
• Butter the foil and add the sliced onion rings. Place the salmon over the onion, and then pour the garlic sauce over the salmon fillets, ensuring they are coated. Add a sprinkle of dill and season to taste.
• Fold the tin foil over the salmon fillets to create parcels, making sure the edges are sealed well.
• Place on the low rack and cook for 15–20 minutes until the fish flakes easily.
• Unwrap and serve with new potatoes and green vegetables.

# Salmon and Prawn Puff Pie

You can prepare this in advance or freeze until needed.

- Preheat the halogen oven using the preheat setting or set the temperature to 210°C.
- In a bowl, combine the crème fraîche, milk and mustard. Season to taste before adding the chopped watercress.
- Place the salmon, prawns and spinach in an ovenproof dish and combine well. Pour the crème fraîche mixture into the dish and combine again.
- Roll out the pastry to a 2–3mm thickness. Using small pie cutters, cut out small circles of about 3cm in diameter.
- Place these pastry circles on the top of the fish mixture, either just around the edges or all over if you prefer. Brush the pastry with a little milk and sprinkle the sesame seeds over the top.
- Place on the low rack and cook for 20–25 minutes until the puff tops have risen and are golden.
- Serve immediately.

300g crème fraîche
250ml milk
1 teaspoon wholegrain mustard
Seasoning to taste
50g watercress, finely chopped
500g salmon fillet pieces
150g prawns
50g baby leaf spinach, shredded
½ pack of puff pastry
Milk for brushing
10g sesame seeds

# Vegetarian

Even if you are not vegetarian, I would strongly recommend you eat a vegetable dish once or twice a week at least. The vegetarian dishes in this chapter are quite conventional. Although I personally love mung beans, you will find the most adventurous ingredient included in this chapter's recipes is tofu – but don't be scared! Some of these dishes can be used as side dishes to accompany a fish or meat meal, while most make wholesome main meals and suppers.

# Eco-Warrior Pie

This is a delicious vegetarian version of a shepherd's pie, using wonderful, fresh vegetables covered in a cheese sauce and topped with sweet potato mash.

SERVES 4–6

3 large potatoes
2 sweet potatoes
1–2 carrots, cut into mini sticks
1–2 leeks, thinly sliced
8–10 small broccoli florets (optional)
25g butter
25g plain flour or cornflour
250ml milk
75–100g mature cheddar, grated
1 teaspoon mustard
Seasoning to taste
1–2 large tomatoes, sliced
1–2 handfuls of spinach leaves

SUITABLE FOR VEGETARIANS

*Note:* If you don't want to make a cheese sauce, you could mix crème fraîche with some mature cheddar. Personally, I like the flavour of the cheese sauce.

- I use a large steamer to prepare the vegetables as I can steam all of them using one hob. First, peel and cut the potatoes into equally-sized chunks or slices (this cuts down on cooking time) and steam them for around 10 minutes. Then add the carrot sticks to the steamer on top of the potatoes and continue steaming. In the last 5–8 minutes of steaming, add the leeks and the broccoli. (This timing assumes that the potatoes will take about 20–25 minutes to steam).
- To make the cheese sauce, melt the butter in a saucepan. Add the flour and stir to form a paste. Gradually add the milk and stir well. I find it best to switch to a balloon whisk at this point as it removes any unwanted lumps. Keep stirring on a medium heat until the sauce thickens. Add the grated cheese, mustard and season to taste. You could use 1 tablespoon of Nutritional Yeast Flakes to create a cheesier taste instead of using more cheese.
- Mash the potatoes with a little milk or butter and season with black pepper.
- Place the tomato slices on the base of an ovenproof dish or 4–6 individual dishes. Cover with a thin layer of uncooked spinach leaves. Then cover the spinach with the leeks, broccoli and carrots and coat with the cheese sauce. Finally add the mash on top.
- Cook in the halogen oven on the low rack at 200°C for 15 minutes until golden.

# Stuffed Mushrooms with Cashew Nut and Parmesan

*This is very tasty and can be used as a side dish or main.*

SERVES 4–6

- Use a food processor to chop the nuts, onion and chestnut mushrooms and leave to one side.
- Combine the breadcrumbs with the grated parmesan and leave to one side until needed. If you are making your own breadcrumbs, simply place the slices of bread in your empty processor and whizz to form breadcrumbs.
- In a sauté or frying pan, add a little olive oil and cook the onion, nuts and mushrooms together for 5 minutes until they begin to soften. Add the yeast extract and stir well.
- Preheat the halogen oven using the preheat setting or set the temperature to 200°C.
- Wash and remove the stalks from the mushrooms. Fill them with the onion/cashew mixture. Finish with a generous layer of the breadcrumb and parmesan mixture.
- Place on the low rack and cook for 15–20 minutes until golden. Serve immediately as a starter or side dish.

SUITABLE FOR VEGETARIANS

100g cashew nuts, finely chopped
1 onion, finely chopped
100g chestnut mushrooms
100g wholemeal breadcrumbs (or 4–5 slices of wholemeal bread to prepare your own)
75g parmesan cheese, grated
Drizzle of olive oil
1 heaped teaspoon yeast extract
4–6 very large, flat mushrooms

# Tofu and Chickpea Burgers

**SERVES 4–6**

I love these burgers. If you like them to taste very spicy, double up on the chillies and add a splash of Tabasco sauce.

1 tin chickpeas, drained

250g or 1 pack of firm tofu

Splash of olive oil

1 onion, finely chopped

1–2 cloves garlic, crushed

1 chilli, finely chopped

1 celery stick, finely chopped

1 teaspoon tomato purée

1–2 teaspoons garam masala

Splash of soy sauce

Seasoning to taste

1 tablespoon home-prepared wholemeal breadcrumbs

1 tablespoon oats

- Put the chickpeas in a large bowl and mash until soft. Add the tofu and continue to mash until the two are thoroughly mixed together.
- Meanwhile, in a little olive oil fry the onion, garlic, chilli and celery until soft. Add to the chickpea and tofu mixture.
- Add the tomato purée, garam masala, soy sauce and seasoning. Stir well before adding the breadcrumbs and oats. (You can make your own home-prepared breadcrumbs by simply whizzing a piece of wholemeal bread in a food processor.)
- Mix thoroughly and form into balls (do this on a floured surface if the mixture is sticky) – the balls should be firm but moist. Use the palm of your hand to flatten the balls into burger shapes.
- Place them in the fridge until you are ready to use them or freeze them in layers. (Separate each layer with parchment to prevent them from sticking together.)
- When you are ready to cook the burgers, brush them lightly with olive oil.
- Turn the halogen oven to 250°C. Place the burgers on the high rack and cook/grill for them for 5–8 minutes on each side until golden.
- Garnish with salad and serve with wholemeal baps.

SUITABLE FOR VEGETARIANS AND VEGANS

# Vegetarian Moussaka

A vegetarian version of this tasty dish.

- Place the aubergine slices in a pan of boiling water for 2 minutes. Remove and pat dry. Leave to one side.
- Meanwhile, heat a little olive oil in a sauté pan and fry the onion and garlic. Add the veggie mince and cook until brown.
- Add the tomatoes, tomato purée, mint, cinnamon and seasoning and cook for another 2–3 minutes.
- Select an ovenproof dish – I normally use a Pyrex or lasagne dish for this recipe – and make sure it fits into your halogen cooker. Preheat your halogen using the preheat setting or set the temperature to 210°C.
- Place a layer of mince in the dish, followed by a layer of aubergine. Continue alternating mince and aubergine, finishing with a layer of mince.
- Mix the crème fraîche with the grated cheese and pour over the final layer of mince. Garnish with a sprinkle of parmesan.
- Place on the low rack in the halogen oven and cook for 20–25 minutes until bubbling.

SUITABLE FOR VEGETARIANS

2–3 aubergines, sliced
Splash of olive oil
1 onion, finely
  chopped
2 cloves garlic,
  crushed
400g veggie mince
1 tin chopped
  tomatoes
2 teaspoons tomato
  purée
1 teaspoon dried mint
2 teaspoons cinnamon
  powder
Seasoning to taste
300ml low fat crème
  fraîche
50g mature cheddar
  or parmesan cheese,
  grated

# Mushroom and Goats' Cheese Bakes

**SERVES 4**

30g butter
4–6 large portobello
  mushrooms
Dash of olive oil
1 red onion, sliced
2 gloves of garlic,
  crushed
1 dessertspoon
  balsamic vinegar
1 dessertspoon brown
  sugar
100g goats' cheese,
  crumbled
Black pepper to
  season

As a child, I never used to like mushrooms but thankfully my tastes have improved and this has now become one of my favourite dishes. You can serve it as a vegetarian roast – that is, as an alternative to a meat roast – or with a salad on a summer's day. The combination of red onion, mushroom and goat's cheese is divine!

- Set the halogen oven to 180°C. Put the butter in a small ovenproof bowl and melt for 2 minutes, but don't let it burn.
- Brush the mushrooms with a little melted butter and place on the low rack for 10 minutes.
- In a frying pan, heat a dash of olive oil. Add the onion and garlic and cook until soft. Add the balsamic vinegar and sugar and cook for another 5 minutes to caramelise the onion.
- Remove the mushrooms from the halogen. Add a little of the onion mix to each mushroom and finish with a crumbling of goats' cheese. Season with black pepper.
- Place back in the oven and cook for another 10 minutes until the goats' cheese is golden.

*Note:* For added variation, why not try crumbling stilton or blue cheese instead of goats' cheese.

SUITABLE FOR VEGETARIANS

# Leek and Cheese Sausages

Another great meat-free alternative to the traditional roast or use them for barbecues.

- Place the breadcrumbs, oats, cheese, leek, egg, milk, thyme and wholegrain mustard in a bowl and mix well. Season to taste. If the mixture is too wet, add more breadcrumbs; if it's too dry, add a little milk. The dough should be firm enough to form thick sausages.
- Put the sausages on a floured sheet of baking parchment and place in the fridge to settle for at least 30 minutes.
- When you are ready to cook the sausages, beat the egg in a bowl and, in a second bowl, mix together the semolina, oatmeal, flour and parmesan. Season to taste.
- Preheat the halogen oven using the preheat setting or set the temperature to 230°C.
- Dip each sausage into the egg, and then into the dry mixture. Ensure they are evenly coated. Place on a greased baking tray or grill tray.
- Place the sausages on the high rack and cook for 5–10 minutes on each side until golden.

SUITABLE FOR VEGETARIANS

125g wholemeal breadcrumbs
30g oats
150g mature cheddar
1 leek, finely chopped
1 egg, beaten
30–40ml milk
1 teaspoon dried thyme
1 teaspoon wholegrain mustard
Seasoning to taste

**Coating:**
1 egg
30g semolina
30g fine oatmeal
20g plain flour
30g parmesan, finely grated
Seasoning to taste

SERVES 4–6

## Basic pizza dough

500g strong bread
    flour
325ml warm water
1 sachet of dried yeast
1 teaspoon brown
    sugar
2 tablespoons olive oil

# Homemade Pizza

To save time, you could make your own pizza dough in advance. Roll it out and place each piece on greased foil or a parchment sheet. Stack the pizza bases on top of each other, cover in cling film or foil and refrigerate until ready to use.

- Sift the flour into a bowl.
- Mix the water, yeast, sugar and oil together. Make sure the sugar is dissolved. Make a well in the middle of the flour and pour this mixture into it.
- Mix thoroughly before transferring the dough onto a floured board. Knead well until the dough springs back when pulled.
- Place the dough in a floured bowl and cover with cling film or a warm, damp cloth until it has doubled in size. This takes about 1 hour.
- Knead again, and divide into individual pizza bases or the size you prefer.
- This dough can be stored in the fridge or freezer until needed.

SUITABLE FOR VEGETARIANS OR VEGANS (DEPENDING ON CHOSEN TOPPINGS)

# Basic pizza toppings

Pizza toppings can be made using pasta sauce or even simple tomato purée mixed with olive oil and herbs. There are no hard and fast rules for pizza toppings so experiment with whatever you fancy and have fun. Below are some suggestions to help you but, really, anything goes!

Tomato and cheese
Pepperoni, mushroom, red onion and cheese
Ham and mushroom
Ham, pineapple and cheese
Chorizo, jalapeno, tomato and cheese
Red onion, black olive, tomato, cheese and red pepper
Roasted vegetables

**Bake your pizza**
- Once your dough has proved, roll it out to the desired thickness and size. Cover it with your desired toppings, starting with the tomato base.
- I normally cook my pizza directly on the lower rack as I like the bottom of the pizza to crisp, but you can place it on a tray or on foil directly on the rack.
- Turn the halogen oven to 200°C and cook for 10–15 minutes until golden.
- Due to the force of the fan, if you have loose toppings you may want to place the high rack face down on top of the pizza – first spray the rack with a little oil to prevent it from sticking. You only need to do this for the first half of the cooking time.

1 punnet of cherry
tomatoes, halved
2–3 cloves of garlic,
crushed
1 red onion, sliced
1 teaspoon salt
1 teaspoon sugar
Handful of crushed
basil leaves
Drizzle of olive oil
1 ball of mozzarella or
80g goats' cheese,
crumbled (omit if
vegan and substitute
with vegan cheese if
desired)

**Basic dough:**
500g strong bread
flour
325ml warm water
1 sachet of dried yeast
1 teaspoon brown
sugar
2 tablespoons olive oil

# Upside Down Pizza Bake

This is a really nice dish and makes a change from the normal pizza. It uses the same principle as an upside down cake. This recipe uses cherry tomatoes, but feel free to use a variety of your choice.

- Place the tomatoes, garlic, onion, salt, sugar, basil and olive oil in a deep-sided baking tray. Ideally choose a round one, so that you can turn this out onto a serving plate when complete, but make sure it fits in your halogen cooker!
- Cook at 130–140°C for 40–50 minutes.
- Meanwhile, prepare the dough. Sift the flour into a bowl. Mix the water, yeast, sugar and oil together. Make sure the sugar is dissolved. Make a well in the middle of the flour and pour this mixture into it.
- Mix thoroughly before transferring the dough onto a floured board. Knead well until the dough springs back when pulled.
- Place the dough in a floured bowl and cover with cling film or a warm, damp cloth until it has doubled in size. This takes about 1 hour.
- Knead again. Roll out to the same size as your baking tray (you will later place the dough inside the tray to form a top). You may have more dough then needed – it depends on how thick you want the crust of the bake. If you have some left over, you can roll it out to make a pizza base – cover this in greased foil or parchment and freeze for another day.
- Remove the baked tomatoes from the halogen oven and turn up to 200°C. Top the tomatoes with the dough – cheese lovers may like to add some crumbled

mozzarella or even goats' cheese onto the tomatoes before adding the dough.
- Place this back into the halogen oven and bake for 15–20 minutes until the top is golden.
- To serve, place a plate, slightly larger than the top of the baking tray, over the dough, face down. Then flip the tray and remove it to display the tomato base on top of the pizza dough.
- Serve with green salad.

SUITABLE FOR VEGETARIANS OR VEGANS

# Sundried Tomato and Goats' Cheese Frittata

SERVES 4–6

- Preheat the halogen oven using the preheat setting or set the temperature to 200°C.
- Beat the eggs well in a large bowl. Add the remaining ingredients and combine. Pour into a well-greased ovenproof dish.
- Place on the low rack and cook for 20–25 minutes until firm.
- Serve hot or cold with salad.

SUITABLE FOR VEGETARIANS

5 eggs
4–5 spring onions, finely chopped
110g goats' cheese, crumbled
4–6 sundried tomatoes, chopped
1 teaspoon mixed dried herbs
Seasoning to taste

# Slow-baked Tomato, Pepper and Basil Soup

**SERVES 4**

8 tomatoes, quartered
1 red pepper, quartered
2–4 cloves of garlic, crushed
Sprinkle of sea salt
Sprinkle of sugar
Small handful of fresh basil leaves (or thyme)
Drizzle of olive oil
500ml vegetable stock or water
1 teaspoon sundried tomato paste
2–3 teaspoons of freshly chopped basil
Seasoning to taste

This is a really tasty soup. If you want a more wholesome version, you could add 50–75g of dried red lentils. Just boil them in water until soft, add with the water and whizz until smooth.

• In your halogen bowl (or you can use a baking tray if you prefer), place the chopped tomatoes, pepper and garlic. Sprinkle with sea salt, sugar, basil leaves (or you can use thyme if you prefer) and drizzle with a light splatter of olive oil. Turn the halogen oven to 160°C and cook for 30 minutes.

• Remove the vegetables from the halogen and mix in the stock. Add more water or stock if necessary (or add the cooked lentils along with the stock or water). Add the tomato paste and chopped basil. Whizz until smooth with an electric hand blender. Season to taste.

• Serve with fresh bread for a tasty lunch or light evening meal.

**SUITABLE FOR VEGETARIANS**

# Roasted Pumpkin Soup

This makes a delicious treat for Halloween or, for an all-year treat, you can use other kinds of squash.

- Preheat the halogen oven using the preheat setting or set the temperature to 200°C.
- Cut the pumpkin, sweet potato and carrots into wedges. Place on a baking tray and lightly brush with oil. Add the onion, garlic and spices and combine well.
- Place on the low rack and bake for 20 minutes.
- Remove the skin from the pumpkin wedges and roughly chop the roasted vegetables. Place them with the onion and seasoning mix in a casserole dish. Add all the remaining ingredients and combine well.
- Place the casserole dish on the low rack. Cover with a lid or with tin foil secured tightly. Cook at 200°C for 30–40 minutes.
- Cool slightly and then use an electric hand blender to purée. Season as required.
- For impressive presentation, use hollowed out pumpkins as serving dishes.

SUITABLE FOR VEGETARIANS AND VEGANS

SERVES 4–6

1 small pumpkin
1 medium sweet potato
1–2 carrots, thickly chopped
Olive oil to brush
1 onion
1–2 garlic cloves, crushed
1 teaspoon grated fresh ginger
1 teaspoon grated nutmeg
1 teaspoon ground coriander
2 sticks of celery
4 tomatoes, peeled and chopped
2 teaspoons of tomato purée (optional)
300–425ml water or stock
15ml lemon juice
Seasoning to taste

# Butternut Squash Stuffed with Mushroom, Cashew Nuts and Goats' Cheese

**SERVES 4–6**

1–2 butternut squash, halved
Drizzle of olive oil
Sprinkle of paprika
Seasoning to taste
1 red onion, finely chopped
2–3 cloves of garlic, crushed
75g cashew nuts, finely chopped
120g mushrooms, finely chopped
110g goats' cheese, crumbled

- Preheat the halogen oven using the preheat setting or set the temperature to 190°C.
- While the oven is heating, halve the butternut squash and remove the seeds. Using a sharp knife, scour the flesh in a criss-cross pattern. Then place the squash on a greased baking tray and brush with olive oil and a sprinkle of paprika. Season to taste.
- Place on the low rack and cook for 30 minutes.
- While that is cooking, place the onion, garlic, cashew nuts and mushrooms in a food processor and whizz until roughly chopped. Alternatively, you can roughly chop by hand.
- Place this chopped mushroom mixture in a sauté pan and fry in a little olive oil for 3–4 minutes. Leave to one side until needed.
- When the butternut squash is soft, remove it from the oven. Scoop out a little of the flesh from each half of the squash to form a small well in the centre. Add this flesh to the mushroom mixture.
- Spoon the mushroom mixture onto the butternut squash. Finish with a scattering of crumbled goats' cheese. Place the squash back in the halogen oven on the low rack for 10–15 minutes until golden.
- Serve with a lovely green salad.

SUITABLE FOR VEGETARIANS

# Vegetable Mornay Bake

SERVES 4–6

- Chop the carrots into sticks, slice the leeks and cut the broccoli and cauliflower into manageable florets. Place in a steamer and cook until the cauliflower is tender but not soft.
- Meanwhile, make the sauce. Melt the butter gently in a saucepan on medium heat (not high!). Add the flour or cornflour and stir well with a wooden spoon. Add the milk a little at a time, continuing to stir to avoid lumps.
- Switch now to a balloon whisk. Continue to stir over a medium heat until the sauce begins to thicken. Add more milk as necessary to get the desired thickness – the sauce should have the consistency of custard.
- If you are using Nutritional Yeast Flakes, add these before the grated cheese as they will reduce the amount of cheese you will need – taste as you go! Add 75g of the cheese and the mustard and stir well. Season with black pepper.
- Preheat the halogen oven using the preheat setting or set the temperature to 210°C.
- When the vegetables are ready, transfer them to an ovenproof dish. Pour the sauce over the vegetables, ensuring they are all covered.
- Mix the breadcrumbs, oats and parmesan together thoroughly. Scatter over the cheese sauce.
- Place the mornay on the low rack. Cook for 15–20 minutes until the top is golden and crispy.

SUITABLE FOR VEGETARIANS

2 carrots
2 leeks
1 small head of broccoli
1 small cauliflower
25g butter
1 tablespoon plain flour or cornflour
500–750ml milk
2 tablespoons Marigold Nutritional Yeast Flakes (optional)
100g mature cheddar, grated (75g for the sauce, 25g for the topping)
½ teaspoon mustard
Black pepper to taste
2–3 tablespoons home-prepared wholemeal breadcrumbs
2 tablespoons oats
25g parmesan cheese

# Leek, Mushroom and Stilton Parcels

**SERVES 4**

Spray of olive oil
1 leek, finely chopped
100g chestnut
   mushrooms,
   quartered
Black pepper to taste
8–12 large cabbage
   leaves
50–75g stilton or blue
   cheese, crumbled
25–40g pine nuts
Seasoning to taste

These flavours were made for each other. This is a great, filling dish, suitable as a main meal for vegetarians or as a side dish or veggie roast alternative.

- Heat the oil in a sauté pan and fry the leek for 2 minutes. Add the mushrooms and fry for 1 minute. Season with black pepper and leave to one side.
- Meanwhile, put the cabbage leaves in a pan of boiling water for 2–3 minutes to soften the leaves. Remove and pat dry with kitchen paper or a clean tea towel.
- Place some of the leek and mushroom filling in the centre of each leaf, then sprinkle over a little of the cheese and the pine nuts and roll into a parcel. If you need to, you can use a wooden cocktail stick to help secure the leaves in place.
- Place the cabbage parcel on a greased square of tin foil. Bring the sides of the foil up to form a well. Add 1 dessertspoon of water and then secure the foil to form a parcel. Repeat this with all the cabbage parcels.
- When all the cabbage leaves are parcelled up, you can place them in and around other food that you are cooking in the halogen, or place them on the low rack. Cook at 230°C for 15 minutes.
- Unwrap and serve.

SUITABLE FOR VEGETARIANS

# Roasted Tomato and Garlic Peppers

I love this dish. You can serve it with a selection of salads or even just some gorgeous homemade bread. If you want to add parmesan, mozzarella or goats' cheese, do so in the last 10 minutes of cooking.

4 red peppers
Olive oil to brush
12 cherry tomatoes, halved
4–6 cloves of garlic, roughly chopped
4–6 sprigs of fresh thyme
1–2 tablespoons olive oil
2 teaspoons balsamic vinegar
Sprinkle of sea salt
Sprinkle of sugar
Sprinkle of black pepper

- Preheat the halogen oven using the preheat setting or set the temperature to 180°C.
- Halve and deseed the peppers. Brush with a little olive oil and place on an ovenproof dish, first making sure it fits well in your halogen.
- Place the tomato halves in the halved peppers. Sprinkle on the garlic and thyme leaves.
- In a bowl or cup, mix the olive oil with the balsamic vinegar. Pour a little of this mixture onto each pepper half. Finish with a sprinkle of sea salt, sugar and black pepper.
- Bake the peppers in the oven on the low rack for 40 minutes until they are soft. If you want to crumble some cheese over the top, do it now and cook again in the oven for 10 more minutes.
- Serve in the dish, mopping up any juice with bread or salad.

SUITABLE FOR VEGETARIANS AND VEGANS

# Leek and Quorn Pie

1 large potato, cubed
2–3 carrots, sliced
Splash of olive oil
1 onion, finely
  chopped
1–2 cloves garlic
  (optional)
2 leeks, finely chopped
200g Quorn
1 tub of quark
3 tablespoons Greek
  yoghurt
75g mature cheddar
  (optional)
Seasoning to taste
Small handful of fresh
  tarragon, chopped,
  or 1 teaspoon dried
½ pack of puff pastry
1 tablespoon milk
Handful of sesame
  seeds for sprinkling

This is a bit like a traditional chicken pie but, using Quorn, it is suitable for vegetarians.

- Steam the chopped potato and carrots for 10 minutes.
- Meanwhile, heat the oil in a large sauté pan and fry the onion, garlic and leeks for 5 minutes to soften.
- Add the Quorn and cook for an additional 5 minutes, then turn off the heat. Add the quark and the yoghurt (and the cheese if you are using it).
- When the potato and carrot are cooked, add them to the leek mix. Season and add the herbs.
- Place the mixture in an ovenproof pie dish, first making sure it fits in the halogen oven. Roll out the pastry to a size larger than required. Wet the edges of the dish with milk or water, and cut thin strips of pastry to place around the edge – dampen again with milk. This will give the top pastry something to hold on to. Cut the top pastry to size and place over the pie. Crimp and seal the edges thoroughly.
- Brush with milk and sprinkle with sesame seeds. Cut 2 holes in the middle of the pastry to allow the pie to breathe.
- Place on the low rack and set the temperature to 200°C. Bake for 20–30 minutes until the pie crust is golden.
- Serve with roast new potatoes and greens.

SUITABLE FOR VEGETARIANS

# Stuffed Peppers with Goats' Cheese

A simple dish – perfect for summer's evenings with a selection of salad dishes.

- Preheat the halogen oven using the preheat setting or set the temperature to 180°C.
- Cut the peppers in half and deseed them. Spray with olive oil, place in an ovenproof dish and bake on the low rack in the halogen oven for 10 minutes.
- Meanwhile, mix the cooked rice or couscous with the spring onions, cherry tomatoes, walnuts and parsley. Season to taste.
- Remove the peppers from the oven and turn up the temperature to 200°C.
- Stuff the peppers with the rice mixture and finish with a layer of goats' cheese.
- Bake on the low rack for 10–15 minutes until the cheese is starting to brown and bubble.

SUITABLE FOR VEGETARIANS

**SERVES 4–6**

4 peppers
Spray of olive oil
400g cooked rice or couscous
Bunch of spring onions, chopped
12 cherry tomatoes, chopped
50g chopped walnuts
Small handful parsley, freshly chopped
Seasoning to taste
125g goats' cheese

# Spinach and Ricotta Lasagne

1 onion, finely
  chopped
1 pot of ricotta
100g mature cheddar,
  grated
150g fresh spinach
  leaves (baby spinach
  is best)
¼ teaspoon grated
  nutmeg
Black pepper to taste
Lasagne sheets
1 jar of pasta sauce
Grated parmesan or
  other cheese for
  topping

We enjoy this dish at least twice a month. It has some great flavours so, even if you aren't vegetarian, give it a try as I am sure it will impress. Unlike most lasagne dishes, it takes minutes to prepare. I recommend using Seeds of Change Cherry Tomato and Parmesan Pasta sauce – it has an authentic homemade taste and look.

• Place the onion, ricotta and cheddar in a bowl and mix well. Add the spinach leaves. (If you place the spinach in a colander and run it under a hot tap for a few seconds, the leaves will soften. This makes the mixing easier.)
• Then add some grated nutmeg and season with black pepper.
• Preheat the halogen oven using the preheat setting or set the temperature to 200°C.
• Place a small layer of the ricotta mixture in the bottom of a lasagne dish, followed by a layer of lasagne sheets. Top with a thin layer of pasta sauce. Continue with a layer of ricotta, then lasagne, and finally the remaining pasta sauce. Add approximately 30ml of water to the empty pasta sauce jar, rinse the jar and pour the water over the top of the lasagne.
• Grate some parmesan or other cheese of your choice onto the lasagne and season.
• Place in the halogen oven on the low rack and cook for 40–50 minutes. If the top starts to get too dark, cover it with tin foil, making sure the foil is secure.
• Serve with potato wedges and salad – delicious!

SUITABLE FOR VEGETARIANS

# Tomato and Mozzarella Puff Tarts

Puff pastry is the busy cook's best friend. You can create your own toppings, but this is a simple favourite to help get you started.

- Roll out the pastry to a 2–3mm thickness and cut it into 4–6 squares. Carefully score around the edge of each square, 1cm from the edge of the pastry – do not cut the pastry, just make a slight indent.
- Preheat the halogen oven using the preheat setting or set the temperature to 210°C.
- In the middle of each pastry square add 1 teaspoon of sundried tomato paste and spread evenly within the scored line. Place pieces of mozzarella and a few leaves of basil inside the scored line. Add a few cherry tomatoes, halved or whole, depending on your preference. Season to taste.
- Place on a lined or well-greased baking tray and place on the high rack. Bake for about 15 minutes until the pastry is golden. If the tarts start to brown before the base is cooked, transfer them to the low rack for a few more minutes.
- Before serving, add a garnish of basil leaves.

SUITABLE FOR VEGETARIANS

SERVES 4

½ pack of readymade puff pastry
4 teaspoons sundried tomato paste
1 pack of mozzarella, sliced
Handful of basil leaves
8–10 cherry tomatoes
Seasoning to taste

# Slow-baked Tomatoes

A batch of ripe
   tomatoes, halved
4 cloves garlic,
   crushed (more if
   preferred)
1 teaspoon salt
1 teaspoon sugar
Sprinkle of balsamic
   vinegar
Drizzle of olive oil
Handful of fresh herbs
   (e.g. basil or
   oregano)

You can use this as a quick and easy pasta sauce, a topping for a pizza, an accompaniment to a meat, fish or vegetable dish, or in a salad. The sweetness of the tomatoes alongside the hit of basil and garlic is truly heaven. I bake this in large batches, especially when I have ripe tomatoes that need using up, or if I see cherry tomatoes on special offer. You can then store it in jars (covered in olive oil) or in an airtight container in the fridge for up to a week.

- Preheat the halogen oven using the preheat setting or set the temperature to 125°C.
- Place the tomatoes in a baking tray. Sprinkle on the garlic, salt, sugar and balsamic vinegar. Finish with a drizzle of olive oil.
- Place in the oven on the low rack for 1 hour.
- When cooked, add a handful of fresh herbs. I prefer oregano or fresh basil.
- Use or store as required.

SUITABLE FOR VEGETARIANS AND VEGANS

# Cheese and Potato Puffs

Perfect for picnics or packed lunches.

- Cook and mash the potatoes.
- Place the potatoes, diced onion, grated carrot and cheese in a bowl and mix thoroughly. Add two thirds of the beaten eggs and the herbs and season well.
- Roll the pastry out on a floured surface until even. Cut into 10cm squares.
- Preheat the halogen oven using the preheat setting or set the temperature to 200°C.
- Place some of the cheese and potato mixture in the centre of each square – do not overfill. Use a little of the remaining beaten egg to brush the edges of the pastry before bringing the edges together to form a triangle. Crimp until sealed.
- Place the pasties on a lined baking tray. Brush with the remaining beaten egg and bake on the low rack for 20–25 minutes until the pastry is golden and flaky.

SUITABLE FOR VEGETARIANS

SERVES 4–6

½–1 pack of puff pastry
3–4 potatoes, cooked and mashed (or use leftover mash)
1 onion, diced
1 carrot, grated
150g mature cheddar, grated
3 eggs, beaten
1 teaspoon mixed herbs (optional)
Seasoning to taste

# Tofu and Stilton Quiche

This quiche is one of my favourites and it is a big hit with meat eaters as well as vegetarians – most don't realise they are eating tofu! It can be adapted for vegans (substitute ingredients are included below if needed).

**SERVES 4–6**

100g plain flour
50g cold butter
5–6 tablespoons cold water
1 box tofu, mashed
125g mature cheddar, grated (you can use vegan cheddar for a vegan quiche)
1 onion, finely chopped
1 tablespoon Marigold Nutritional Yeast Flakes (optional but gives a cheesier taste and is full of B vitamins)
Dash of milk (if needed)
Seasoning to taste
40–50g stilton or blue cheese

- Make the pastry. Place the flour in a large bowl and add small pieces of the chilled butter. Using your fingertips, rub the butter into the flour until the whole mix resembles breadcrumbs. Add the water (a little at a time) and mix until dough is formed. Wrap the dough in cling film and place in the fridge to cool until needed.
- Preheat the halogen oven using the preheat setting or set the temperature to 200°C.
- Roll out the pastry on a floured surface to the size and thickness needed to line a 23cm greased flan tin. Place a sheet of baking parchment over the pastry and cover with baking beans.
- Bake in the oven for 10 minutes. Remove the baking beans and parchment and cook for a further 5 minutes. Remove the pastry case from the halogen and turn the oven down to 180°C.
- Meanwhile, mash the tofu thoroughly. Add grated cheese, onion and Nutritional Yeast Flakes if you are including them. If the mixture is too dry, add a dash of milk and mix well. Season well before pouring into the pastry case. Cover with a sprinkling of crumbled stilton and then place the tin on the high rack.
- Bake in the oven for 20 minutes until golden.

SUITABLE FOR VEGETARIANS

# Spinach and Feta Pie

Serve this with a selection of fresh salads and new potatoes –
it's the perfect dish for a summer's evening.

- Preheat the halogen oven using the preheat setting or
  set the temperature to 200°C.
- Melt the butter in a saucepan or place it in a bowl in
  your halogen oven to melt, though make sure it
  doesn't burn.
- Layer 3 sheets of pastry in the base of your pie dish
  (first making sure the dish fits comfortably within
  your halogen oven). Brush butter between the sheets
  and allow them to hang over the edge of the dish to
  give you enough pastry to form the sides of the pie.
- Place a thin layer of spinach leaves and then a layer of
  crumbled feta. Season with black pepper and nutmeg.
  Repeat this, finishing with the feta layer.
- Cover with more filo sheets, again brushing with
  butter. Bring the edges together to form a crust and
  remove any excess pastry.
- Brush with butter and sprinkle with sesame seeds.
- Place on the low rack and bake for 30–40 minutes
  until golden.

SUITABLE FOR VEGETARIANS

**SERVES 4–6**

40g butter
6 sheets of filo pastry
400g baby leaf
  spinach, roughly
  torn
250g feta cheese,
  crumbled
Black pepper to
  season
¼ teaspoon grated
  nutmeg
Sesame seeds to
  sprinkle

# Baked Mushroom Rarebit

**SERVES 4–6**

30g butter
4–6 large portobello
  mushrooms
2 tablespoons milk
100g mature cheddar
1 teaspoon mustard
Seasoning to taste

Cheese and mushrooms … yummy! Serve as a main dish with vegetables or as a snack with toast triangles.

- Set the halogen oven to 180°C. Put the butter in a small ovenproof bowl and melt it in the halogen for 2–3 minutes, but don't let it burn.
- Brush the mushrooms with a little melted butter and place them on the low rack for 8–10 minutes.
- In a saucepan, add the milk, remaining butter, cheese and mustard. Stir until the ingredients are dissolved and thick. Be careful not to have the temperature too high or it will stick and burn.
- Pour the cheesy mixture over the mushrooms. Season to taste. Place on the high rack and cook on high heat/grill (250–260°C) for 5 minutes until golden and bubbling.

SUITABLE FOR VEGETARIANS

# Vegetable Cheesy Cobbler

SERVES 4

- Chop the vegetables and place them in a steamer. Steam until soft.
- Meanwhile, make the sauce. Melt the butter gently in a saucepan on medium heat (not high!). Add the flour or cornflour and stir well with a wooden spoon. Add the milk a little at a time, continuing to stir to avoid lumps.
- Switch now to a balloon whisk. Continue to stir over a medium heat until the sauce begins to thicken.
- If you are using Nutritional Yeast Flakes, add these before the grated cheddar as they will reduce the amount of cheese you will need – taste as you go! Add the cheddar and mustard and stir well. Season with black pepper.
- Preheat the oven using the preheat setting or set the temperature to 180°C.
- Place the self-raising flour and parmesan in a bowl and season to taste. Create a well in the centre and add the oil and yoghurt. Stir well to form a dough.
- Roll out the dough on a floured surface to a 3–5cm thickness. Use pastry cutters to create scones.
- Place the vegetables in the base of an ovenproof dish. Pour over the cheese sauce and finish with the scones placed around the edge of the dish. Brush the scones with a little milk and sprinkle with sesame seeds. Then place the dish in the oven and cook on the low rack for 25–30 minutes.

SUITABLE FOR VEGETARIANS

2 leeks, finely sliced
2 carrots, cut into sticks
½ head of broccoli
½ head of cauliflower
25g butter
25g plain flour (or cornflour)
500–750ml milk
2 tablespoons Marigold Nutritional Yeast Flakes (optional)
100g mature cheddar, grated
½ teaspoon mustard
Seasoning to taste
100g self-raising flour
40g parmesan cheese, finely grated
2 tablespoons olive oil
75ml natural yoghurt
Sprinkle of sesame seeds

# Roasted Mediterranean-style Vegetables

The halogen lends itself so well to roasting. This is a lovely dish and can be used a bit like a ratatouille.

**SERVES 4–6**

2–3 red onions, quartered

1 whole bulb of garlic, broken into cloves

2 aubergines, cut into thick chunks

1 fennel bulb, quartered, then halved again

2 red peppers, quartered

Drizzle of olive oil

3 tablespoons balsamic vinegar

Small handful fresh basil leaves

Sprigs of fresh thyme

Seasoning to taste

4–6 vine tomatoes

Sprinkle of sugar

- Preheat the halogen oven using the preheat setting or set the temperature to 210°C.
- Place all the prepared vegetables, except the tomatoes, into a roasting/baking or ovenproof tray.
- Drizzle with olive oil and balsamic and scatter with basil leaves and thyme sprigs. Season to taste.
- Place on the low rack and cook for 20 minutes.
- Sprinkle the tomatoes with a very small amount of sugar. Then remove the pan and add the tomatoes. Stir the vegetables, ensuring they are re-coated in oil and balsamic.
- Turn the temperature down to 180°C. Place the vegetables back into the halogen on the low rack for another 20 minutes until they are cooked.

SUITABLE FOR VEGETARIANS AND VEGANS

# Ratatouille and Feta Gratin

*I love the crispy bake topping of this dish.*

- Preheat the halogen oven using the preheat setting or turn the temperature to 210°C.
- Place all the prepared vegetables in an ovenproof dish. Add the olive oil, sugar, balsamic vinegar, wine, herbs and seasoning. Combine to ensure all the vegetables are covered in a little oil.
- Bake on the low rack for 20–30 minutes until the vegetables are soft.
- While this is cooking, mix together the breadcrumbs, oats and parmesan. Season to taste.
- Remove the vegetables from the oven and stir in the feta cheese. Finish with the breadcrumb mix.
- Return to the low rack and cook for another 15 minutes until golden.

SUITABLE FOR VEGETARIANS

SERVES 4

1 aubergine, diced
1 red onion, sliced
2 cloves of garlic, crushed
1 red pepper, roughly diced
1 courgette, diced
8 ripe tomatoes, quartered (or use tinned if you prefer)
Olive oil
Sprinkle of sugar
2–3 teaspoons balsamic vinegar
100ml red wine
Sprigs of thyme
Small handful of bay leaves
Seasoning to taste
75g wholemeal breadcrumbs
50g oats
50g parmesan cheese, grated
120g feta cheese, crumbled

**SERVES 4–6**

4–6 beefsteak
 tomatoes
Drizzle of olive oil
1 red onion, finely
 chopped
2–3 cloves of garlic,
 crushed
½ red pepper
20g pine nuts
Small handful of basil
 leaves, chopped
50–75g couscous
Seasoning to taste
40g mozzarella,
 crumbled

# Stuffed Tomatoes

Perfect for a summer's evening with minted new potatoes and various salad dishes – I can almost smell the freshly mowed grass!

- Preheat the halogen oven using the preheat setting or turn the temperature to 180°C.
- Carefully cut off the tops of the tomatoes and scoop out the flesh. Chop the removed tops finely and place them along with the flesh in a bowl. Place the tomato shells on a baking tray and leave to one side until needed.
- In a sauté pan, fry the onion and the garlic in a little olive oil for a couple of minutes. Then add the red pepper and cook until soft.
- Remove from the heat and add to the bowl of tomato flesh. Add the pine nuts and basil leaves.
- Re-hydrate the couscous following the instructions on the pack, then add it to the bowl. Season to taste and stir well to combine all the ingredients.
- Place this mixture in your tomato shells, finishing with some crumbled mozzarella. Finish with black pepper before placing on the low rack and cooking for 25–30 minutes.

SUITABLE FOR VEGETARIANS

# Spicy Stuffed Butternut Squash

If you have not tried butternut squash before, give it a go – it is really delicious and this is a very simple dish to prepare.

- Preheat the halogen oven using the preheat setting or set the temperature to 190°C.
- While the oven is heating, halve the butternut squash and remove the seeds. Using a sharp knife, scour the flesh in a criss-cross pattern. Place the squash on a greased baking tray. Brush with olive oil and a sprinkle of paprika.
- Place on the low rack and cook for 30 minutes.
- Meanwhile, fry in a sauté pan the onion, garlic and chilli until they start to soften. Add the curry powder and red pepper and cook for another couple of minutes before adding all remaining ingredients, apart from the cheese.
- Cook for another 5 minutes making sure the ingredients are well combined. Leave to one side.
- When the butternut squash is soft, remove it from the oven. Scoop out a little of the flesh to form a small well in the centre of each half of the butternut squash. Add this flesh to the bean mixture and then spoon the bean mixture into the squash.
- If you like cheesy chilli flavours, scatter grated cheese over the top of each squash before placing back in the halogen oven. Cook on the low rack for 10–15 minutes until golden.
- Serve with a lovely green salad.

SUITABLE FOR VEGETARIANS AND VEGANS

1–2 butternut squash
Brush of olive oil
Sprinkle of paprika
1 red onion, finely chopped
2–3 cloves of garlic, crushed
1 chilli, finely chopped
1–2 teaspoons curry powder
1 red pepper, finely chopped
1 tin chopped tomatoes
1 tin mixed beans, drained
Small handful of coriander leaves, finely chopped
Seasoning to taste
Grated cheese (optional – omit for a vegan version)

# Spinach and Ricotta Cannelloni

150g fresh baby leaf
 spinach (or 300g
 frozen spinach)
1 tub of ricotta
¼ teaspoon grated
 nutmeg
6–8 cannelloni tubes
 or lasagne sheets
1 small red onion
2 cloves of garlic,
 crushed
Drizzle of olive oil
1 tin chopped
 tomatoes
75ml red wine
Handful of freshly
 chopped basil leaves
Seasoning to taste
Grated parmesan to
 sprinkle

This is such a simple dish to make, but it looks impressive and tastes even better!

- Place the spinach in a colander and run under hot water for a couple of minutes to soften the leaves. If you are using frozen spinach, allow it to defrost before moving on to the next step.
- In a bowl, mix the ricotta, spinach and nutmeg together. Using a teaspoon, fill the cannelloni tubes with the ricotta mixture. Place the stuffed tubes in an ovenproof dish in a single layer. (If you want to speed up the cooking time, you can use fresh cannelloni tubes. If you are using dried lasagne sheets, first cook them in boiling water for 5–8 minutes and then drain. Add the ricotta mixture to one end of the sheets. Roll them up firmly to form tubes and place them seal-side down on the bottom of the ovenproof dish.)
- Preheat the halogen oven using the preheat setting or set the temperature to 190°C.
- Whilst the oven is preheating, fry the onion and garlic in a little olive oil to help soften. Add the tomatoes, wine, basil leaves and seasoning and cook for a couple of minutes before pouring over the cannelloni.
- Sprinkle with parmesan before placing on the low rack. Cook for 35–40 minutes until the cannelloni is cooked. (This takes 20–25 minutes if you are using fresh pasta or lasagne sheets as described above.)
- Serve with some garlic bread and green salad.

SUITABLE FOR VEGETARIANS

# Roasted Vegetable and Chickpea Salad

**SERVES 4-6**

You can prepare the roasted vegetables in advance and leave them in the fridge until needed.

- Preheat the halogen oven using the preheat setting or set the temperature to 200°C.
- Prepare the onion, peppers and tomatoes (leaving aside the cherry tomatoes for now) and place on a baking tray. Drizzle with olive oil, sprinkle with sugar and a little salt. Add the thyme and rosemary leaves.
- Place on the low rack and cook for 20 minutes until the vegetables are soft.
- Remove from the heat and place in a bowl. (You can serve this dish hot or cold – it's your choice, but I prefer it hot.) Add the drained chickpeas, halved cherry tomatoes and chopped mint leaves.
- In a jug, mix the 2 tablespoons of olive oil, white wine vinegar, crushed garlic and lemon juice. Season to taste. Pour this over the vegetable mixture and combine well.

SUITABLE FOR VEGETARIANS AND VEGANS

12 small red onions, cut into wedges
2 peppers, thickly sliced
4 tomatoes, quartered
Drizzle of olive oil
1 teaspoon sugar
Sprinkle of salt
Small handful of rosemary and thyme sprigs
1 tin chickpeas, drained
4–6 cherry tomatoes, halved
Small handful of fresh mint leaves, chopped
2 tablespoons olive oil
2 tablespoons white wine vinegar
2 cloves of garlic, crushed
Juice of ½ a lemon
Seasoning to taste

# Slow Cook Basil and Tomato Pasta Bake with Feta

**SERVES 4**

8–10 ripe tomatoes, quartered

3–4 cloves of garlic, crushed

2 red onions, cut into wedges

1–2 red peppers, thickly sliced

Handful of basil leaves

Drizzle of olive oil

1 dessertspoon balsamic vinegar

1 teaspoon sugar

1 teaspoon salt

300g penne pasta

200g feta cheese, cut into cubes

Olives, chopped (optional)

This dish was invented by accident – while I was preparing slow-baked tomatoes for a soup, my family then declared they would rather have pasta for dinner! Fortunately it turned out well and is now a family favourite. I hope you enjoy it. If there is any leftover slow-cooked tomatoes, store them in the fridge and use as a pizza topping.

- Preheat the halogen oven using the preheat setting or set the temperature to 170°C.
- In an ovenproof dish, combine the tomatoes, garlic, onion, peppers and half the basil leaves. Drizzle with oil, balsamic vinegar and sprinkle with sugar and a little salt.
- Place on the low rack and cook for 30 minutes.
- Timing is everything so, when you are ready to serve, cook the pasta as per the instructions on the packet. It will not hurt to cook the tomato mixture in advance and leave it until you are ready to continue. Just reheat the tomatoes 5 minutes before the pasta is cooked.
- Drain the cooked pasta and place with the tomato mixture in an ovenproof dish. Stir in the feta cubes and olives. Place back in the halogen oven on the low rack and cook for 10 minutes at 190°C.
- Serve with a green salad.

SUITABLE FOR VEGETARIANS

# Roasted Butternut, Spinach and Goats' Cheese Layer

This may take a little time to prepare but, other than chopping, the halogen does the hard work for you. It tastes amazing and will impress even the most ardent meat eaters!

- Preheat the halogen oven using the preheat setting or set the temperature to 210°C.
- Whilst the oven is heating, prepare your vegetables. In a pestle and mortar, roughly grind the coriander and cumin seeds.
- Place the squash slices on a baking tray and drizzle with olive oil. Sprinkle with the coriander seeds, cumin and chilli.
- Place on the low rack and roast for 15 minutes. Remove and add the onion and garlic. Place back in the oven and cook for another 15 minutes.
- Meanwhile, you can prepare the rest of the layers. Rinse the spinach leaves under a hot tap to soften the leaves. Place the leaves in a bowl and mix in the ricotta. Season to taste and leave to one side.
- Remove the squash from the oven. Drain off any excess oil and combine the squash, onion and garlic together. Place half of this in the bottom of an ovenproof dish.
- Add a layer of the spinach and ricotta mix. Follow this with a layer of sliced tomatoes, the rest of the squash, the ricotta mixture, pine nuts and finish with the crumbled goats' cheese.
- Place on the low rack and bake for 20 minutes.
- Serve with a selection of delicious salads.

SUITABLE FOR VEGETARIANS

1 butternut squash, peeled, deseeded and sliced
Drizzle of olive oil
2 teaspoons coriander seeds
1 teaspoon cumin
1–2 chillies, finely chopped (depending on desired strength)
2 red onions, sliced
3–4 cloves of garlic, chopped
50–75g baby leaf spinach
1 tub of ricotta
Seasoning to taste
1–2 ripe tomatoes, sliced
25g pine nuts
110g goats' cheese, crumbled

SERVES 4–6

1 sweet potato, diced
1 potato, diced
2 carrots, diced
Drizzle of olive oil
1 onion, finely
    chopped
2–3 cloves of garlic,
    finely chopped
1 red pepper, diced
1 stick of celery, diced
1 tin chopped
    tomatoes
200ml vegetable stock
1–2 handfuls of fresh
    baby leaf spinach
Small handful of
    mixed fresh herbs
Seasoning to taste
175g plain flour
75g butter (or use
    vegan spread)
50g mature cheddar
    (for the vegan
    version, omit the
    cheese or substitute
    with a sprinkle of
    Marigold Nutritional
    Yeast Flakes or vegan
    cheese)

# Vegetable Crumble

This is a very filling one-pot dish packed with goodness. Serve it on its own or with a salad for a perfect meal.

• Prepare your vegetables. Place the potatoes and carrots in a steamer and steam for 10 minutes to soften them.
• Meanwhile, place olive oil in sauté pan and sauté the onion and garlic until it starts to soften. Add the pepper, celery, chopped tomatoes, vegetable stock, spinach and herbs and cook for 10 minutes.
• Preheat the halogen oven using the preheat setting or set the temperature to 180°C.
• Add the potatoes and carrots to the tomato mixture and season to taste. Pour this into an ovenproof dish, first making sure it fits well in your halogen oven.
• Put the flour into a bowl and rub in the butter to form a texture similar to breadcrumbs. Add the grated cheese and season. Sprinkle this over the vegetable base. Place the crumble on the low rack and cook for 20 minutes until golden and bubbling. Serve immediately.

SUITABLE FOR VEGETARIANS OR VEGANS

# Sausage in Redcurrant and Onion Gravy with Veggie Mash

**SERVES 4**

There is no reason why vegetarians can't enjoy traditional favourites like sausage and mash. Roast the sausages with redcurrant jelly and red onions before making a rich gravy and serving with a vegetable mash.

- Preheat the halogen oven using the preheat setting or set the temperature to 210°C.
- Place the potato, carrot and sweet potato in a steamer and cook until soft and ready to mash.
- Meanwhile, drizzle some olive oil in the bottom of an ovenproof dish. Add the sausages, garlic, onion and redcurrant jelly. Combine well, ensuring the jelly is mixed in.
- Place on the low rack and cook for 20 minutes. A couple of times during cooking, stir with a wooden spoon to combine the flavours again.
- When the sausages have cooked and browned, add the wine and gravy or stock. Combine well. If you need to thicken, place a little water in a cup and add 1 teaspoon of cornflour. Stir until combined and then add to the gravy, stirring well. Leave to thicken naturally for a few minutes.
- Place back in the oven and cook for another 15 minutes.
- Mash the potato and veg, adding a little butter or milk.
- Serve together with green vegetables.

SUITABLE FOR VEGETARIANS AND VEGANS

4–5 potatoes, diced
2 carrots, diced
1 sweet potato, diced
Drizzle of olive oil
6–8 good quality vegetarian sausages
1 clove of garlic, crushed
1–2 red onions, sliced
1 tablespoon redcurrant jelly
150ml red wine
300ml gravy or stock, heated
25g butter or 75ml milk (or use vegan spread or soya milk)

100g lentils
2 carrots, diced in
small cubes
1 bay leaf
250–350ml water
Drizzle of olive oil
1 onion, finely
chopped
2 cloves of garlic,
crushed
1 pepper, red or
green, finely
chopped
50g oats
50g cooked brown rice
1 teaspoon mixed
herbs
Seasoning to taste
2–3 ripe tomatoes,
chopped
1–2 teaspoons
sundried tomato
paste

# Lentil Loaf

Traditionally this loaf would have been used instead of meat to make up a vegetarian roast, but you can also slice it to accompany most meals. Serve with a creamy cheese sauce or, for a vegan version, opt for a herby tomato and basil sauce.

• Preheat the halogen oven using the preheat setting or set the temperature to 180°C.
• Place the lentils, carrots and bay leaf in a saucepan of water. Boil for 10 minutes. Then drain and place in a bowl, reserving the water in case it is needed later.
• Meanwhile, while the lentils are boiling, fry the onion in a little olive oil. Add the garlic and pepper. Once cooked, place in the bowl with the lentils and carrots.
• Add the remaining ingredients to form a thick mixture that is not too wet. Use the retained stock if the mixture is too dry.
• Pour into a well-greased or lined 1lb loaf tin and bake on the low rack for 30 minutes.
• Leave to stand for 10 minutes before turning out onto a plate.

*Note:* For variation, place half the mixture in your loaf tin, then add some cheese sauce or crumbled feta, mozzarella or even stilton. Place the remaining mixture over the cheese and press down firmly. Bake as given above.

# Cheese Scones

I love cheese scones, especially when made with mature cheese, a touch of cayenne pepper and paprika. Enjoy these hot or cold but best to be eaten on the day.

- Preheat the halogen oven using the preheat setting or set the temperature to 210°C.
- Sift the flour into a bowl. Add the cayenne pepper and mustard and season to taste.
- Add the butter and rub to form breadcrumbs. Add the grated cheese and combine well.
- Gradually add the milk to form a dough that is firm but not wet.
- Place the dough on a floured board, and press out to a 3–4cm thickness. Cut the scones out with a pastry cutter and place them on a greased baking tray. Brush with milk.
- Place in the halogen oven on the low rack for 10 minutes. Once cooked, place the scones on a cooling rack or serve warm!

*Note:* There is no reason why you can't add finely chopped onion. Non-vegetarians might like to try adding some chopped cooked bacon or pancetta for a delicious savoury scone. Experiment by adding your favourite herbs. You can also use this recipe to form a cobbler topping on a savoury dish.

SUITABLE FOR VEGETARIANS

200g self-raising flour
1 teaspoon mustard powder
Pinch of cayenne pepper
Seasoning to taste
30g butter
60g mature cheddar
125ml milk

# Quorn Italianano

**SERVES 4**

Olive oil
1 onion
2–3 cloves garlic,
   crushed
1 red pepper, diced
6 Quorn Fillets or
   quorn pieces
75g button
   mushrooms
2 teaspoons paprika
1 tin of chopped
   tomatoes
2 teaspoons sundried
   tomato paste
200ml red wine
200ml stock or water
150g button
   mushrooms
Small handful of fresh
   basil, chopped
Seasoning to taste

Meat eaters can opt for the Chicken Italianano dish found in
the Meat Chapter, but this is a veggie variation that is
delicious. Quorn is not suitable for vegans.

- In a large sauté pan, fry the onion and garlic in a
  dash of olive oil for 2 minutes. Add the peppers and
  cook for another 2 minutes.
- Add the quorn, mushrooms and paprika. Stir,
  cooking gently for 5 minutes.
- Add all the remaining ingredients. Cook for another
  couple of minutes.
- Pour this into a casserole dish that fits in the Halogen
  Oven. Cover the pan with a lid and cook 180°C for
  30 minutes.
- Serve with small roast or sauté potatoes and
  vegetables.

SUITABLE FOR VEGETARIANS

# Quorn and Mushroom Casserole

A wholesome meal that everyone loves. Quorn is not suitable for Vegans

**SERVES 4**

- 1 teaspoon dried tarragon (or a handful of fresh tarragon)
- Heat a little olive oil in a sauté pan and cook the garlic, leeks and spring onions for 2–3 minutes. Add the quorn pieces and the mushrooms and cook for a further 5 minutes.
- Place the quorn mixture in your casserole dish (make sure this fits in the Halogen Oven). Add the wine and stock to the dish.
- Mix the cornflour with 10ml of water in a cup to form a smooth paste and add to the quorn pot.
- Add all the remaining ingredients. If you are using fresh tarragon, add half now and retain half to add in the last 10 minutes of cooking.
- Cook at 180°C for 30 minutes. If the casserole starts to form a skin on the top you can pop on the casserole lid, or wrap securely a piece of tin foil over the top of the dish.

SUITABLE FOR VEGETARIANS

A drizzle or spray of olive oil
1–2 cloves garlic
2 leeks, finely chopped
6 spring onions, finely chopped
300g quorn pieces
175g mushrooms
200ml white wine
300ml vegetable stock
1 teaspoon cornflour
1 teaspoon paprika
100g French beans

# Desserts

Who can resist a delicious dessert to finish off a meal? In restaurants I have often felt like opting for a starter and dessert and omitting the main meal altogether. Desserts don't always have to be calorie-laden feasts (although they are great occasionally!). In this chapter you will find some desserts that are surprisingly good for you. My personal favourite is the Healthy Brûlèe which literally takes minutes to make.

# Upside Down Strawberry Cheesecake

I am a big fan of cheesecake and this is a yummy variation of the classic recipe.

**SERVES 4–6**

150–200g strawberries, quartered or thickly sliced
1 tub of cream cheese
1 tub of Greek yoghurt
2–3 tablespoons crème fraîche
1 teaspoon vanilla paste
Juice and zest of 1–2 lemons
6–8 digestive biscuits
2–3 tablespoons brown sugar

- Prepare the strawberries and place them in the bottom of an ovenproof serving dish. (The dish needs to be big enough for 4–6 servings, but make sure it fits in your halogen oven.)
- Combine the cream cheese, yoghurt and crème fraîche. Add the vanilla paste and stir well.
- Roughly peel the lemon with a vegetable peeler to remove the zest. Chop this finely before adding to the cream cheese mixture. Also add the juice of the lemon. Taste and add another lemon if you prefer a more zesty flavour.
- When you are happy with the mix, carefully spoon it over the strawberries.
- Place the biscuits in a plastic jug or bowl. Using the end of a wooden rolling pin, gently bash the biscuits to form biscuit crumbs. (You could use a food processor but I find this method saves washing up!)
- Sprinkle the biscuit crumbs over the cream cheese mixture and follow with a sprinkle of brown sugar.
- Place in the fridge for at least 30 minutes until you are ready to serve the cheesecake.
- Turn on the halogen oven to 250°C. Place the cheesecake on the high rack for 3 minutes and then serve.

*Note:* As with the Crème Brûlèe recipe later in this chapter, you can use frozen or fresh raspberries for the cheesecake. You could also try mixed summer fruit or blueberries. If you are using frozen fruit, use the halogen's defrost/thaw setting and place the fruit in the ovenproof serving dish on the low rack for 10 minutes before adding the cream cheese mixture.

SUITABLE FOR VEGETARIANS

# Baked Cinnamon Apples

SERVES 4

A traditional autumnal treat.

- Preheat the halogen oven using the preheat setting or set the temperature to 220°C.
- Wash and core the apples, leaving the skins intact. Mix the honey with the boiling water and the cinnamon. Stir until dissolved.
- Place the apples on a baking tray or ovenproof dish and add the 2 tablespoons of water to the dish. Brush the apples with the honey mixture.
- Stuff the cores of the apples with mincemeat. Finish with a sprinkling of brown sugar.
- Bake in the oven for 30–40 minutes until soft.
- Serve with low-fat crème fraîche or natural yoghurt.

4 Bramley apples
2 teaspoons runny
  honey
10ml boiling water
2–3 teaspoons ground
  cinnamon
2 tablespoons water
Mincemeat
Brown sugar

SUITABLE FOR VEGETARIANS

4–6 ripe pears
400-500ml mulled
   wine
1 orange, thickly sliced
175g sugar

# Mulled Baked Pears

This can be prepared in advance. Serve with vanilla ice-cream or a dollop of crème fraîche.

- Preheat your Halogen Oven using the preheat setting or set temperature to 160°C.
- Place the wine in a saucepan and heat up gently. Add half the sugar and stir until dissolved.
- Peel your pears retaining the stalk if possible. Cut the bottom off the pear allowing it to stand without falling over.
- Place the orange slices in the bottom of the ovenproof dish, (The smaller the dish, the more of the pear will be covered in wine).
- Place the pears in the dish, (you can sit the pears on top of the orange slices or lie flat to allow more of the pears to be covered in the liquid).
- Pour the wine over the pears. Sprinkle the pears with the remainder of the sugar.
- Cover securely with foil and place on the low rack for 1 hour.
- Uncover and spoon the wine back over the pears. Add more wine or red grape juice if necessary.
- Cook uncovered for another 20 minutes until the pears are soft.
- Place the pears on a plate and drizzle over with the juice. Serve with a dollop of cream, Greek yoghurt or crème fraîche.

SUITABLE FOR VEGETARIANS AND VEGANS

# Baked Raspberry Cheesecake

If you don't want raspberry, you could opt for other berries such as blueberry or even sultanas soaked in liqueur.

- In a bowl, cut the butter into small pieces and then add flour and rub fat into it until fine breadcrumbs.
- Mix together the sugar and egg yolks and 2 tablespoons of water.
- Add to flour and mix to a soft dough, if necessary add a tablespoon of water.
- Spread the mixture into a greased or lined tin with a spring clip, pressing down firmly. Make sure the tin fits in the Halogen Oven! Sprinkle the raspberries on top of the dough.
- Beat the egg whites until stiff, add the sugar and beat for one minute.
- In a bowl beat the cream cheese and vanilla paste/essence and then fold in the egg whites.
- Spread the mixture over the raspberries. Place on the low rack in the Halogen Oven. Turn temperature to 180°C and bake for 35-45 minutes until firm and golden.
- Leave to cool and serve with a scattering of fresh raspberries to garnish.

SUITABLE FOR VEGETARIANS

SERVES 6

115g butter
250g self-raising flour
100g caster sugar
3 egg yolks
100g Raspberries

**For the topping:**
3 egg whites
50g Sugar
400g cream cheese
1 teaspoon vanilla essence or paste

# Gooseberry Betty

SERVES 4–6

750g gooseberries
1–2 tablespoons sugar
1–2 tablespoons water
125g breadcrumbs
50g oats
2 teaspoons ground
   cinnamon
100g butter (for a
   vegan version, use
   dairy-free
   margarine)
3 tablespoons golden
   syrup

I adore the taste of gooseberries and this makes a wonderfully satisfying dessert. A great variation to the standard fruit crumble.

• Preheat the halogen oven using the preheat setting or set the temperature to 190°C.
• Place the gooseberries in an ovenproof dish. Sprinkle with the sugar and water. Place on the low rack and cook for 10 minutes. Stir and press the gooseberries slightly to help 'burst' them a little. Cook for another 5 minutes before removing from the oven.
• Whilst the gooseberries are cooking, combine the breadcrumbs, oats and cinnamon. Place this mixture over the top of the fruit.
• Place the butter and syrup in an ovenproof dish and melt using the heat from the halogen oven – do not allow it to burn. Once melted, pour this mixture over the crumble mixture.
• Return gooseberry betty to the halogen's low rack. Cook for another 15–20 minutes until the top is golden.
• Serve with a dollop of crème fraîche or vanilla ice-cream.

SUITABLE FOR VEGETARIANS AND VEGANS

# Baked Bananas with Dark Chocolate Sauce

This is so simple but tastes amazing.

- Preheat the halogen oven using the preheat setting or set the temperature to 180°C.
- Place the bananas in an ovenproof tray in their skins and bake on the low rack for 10 minutes, or until the skin goes completely black.
- Meanwhile, melt the chocolate, butter, honey and cocoa in a bowl over a saucepan of water or a bain marie.
- When you are ready to serve, pour the chocolate mixture over the bananas and finish with a generous dollop of crème fraîche or ice-cream.

SUITABLE FOR VEGETARIANS

**SERVES 4**

4 bananas
120g bar of dark chocolate
25g butter
1–2 tablespoons honey
1 tablespoon cocoa

# Winter Spice Crumble

600g chopped fruit (I
use rhubarb,
Bramley apples and
plums or apple
mixed with frozen
forest fruits)
100–150ml red wine
or orange juice
100g sugar
3 teaspoons ground
cinnamon
1 teaspoon allspice
150ml plain flour
50g oats
1 teaspoon mixed
spice
75g butter (for a
vegan version, use
dairy-free
margarine)
40g sliced almonds

If you love the flavour of cinnamon and allspice, this is the
pudding for you. Serve with vanilla ice-cream.

- Preheat the halogen oven using the preheat setting or
  set the temperature to 180°C.
- Place the fruit in a saucepan and add the wine or
  orange juice and 50g of the sugar. Cook gently for
  5–8 minutes to begin softening the fruit.
- Mix in the cinnamon and allspice and stir well,
  pressing the fruit a little with your spoon to help
  break or soften. Pour into an ovenproof dish, first
  making sure it fits well in your halogen oven.
- In a bowl, combine the flour, oats and mixed spice.
  Add the butter and rub until it forms a texture similar
  to breadcrumbs. Add the remaining 50g of brown
  sugar and almonds and combine well.
- Pour this over the fruit base, making sure it is spread
  evenly.
- Place the crumble on the low rack and cook for 20
  minutes.
- Serve with a dollop of vanilla ice-cream.

SUITABLE FOR VEGETARIANS AND VEGANS

# Lemon Saucy Pudding

SERVES 4–6

- Using a food processor or cake mixer, beat the butter and sugar together until creamy.
- Using a sharp vegetable peeler, peel the zest from 2 or 3 lemons (depending on your desired lemony intensity). The peeler magically peels the zest and leaves the white pith behind. Finely chop the zest and add to the beaten sugar and butter mixture.
- Add the egg yolks, vanilla and lemon juice. Beat well before adding the flour and milk. This will form quite a runny batter. Give it a thorough stir to make sure the mixer has not left anything on the edges of the bowl.
- Meanwhile, in a clean bowl, beat the egg whites until they form soft peaks. Fold gently into the batter.
- Line a baking dish with butter. I use a Pyrex baking dish but you could use individual ramekin dishes. Pour in the mixture.
- Pour hot water into your halogen oven up to approximately 3cm (1inch) from the bottom. Then place the baking dish in the water to create a bain marie. If you prefer and have room, you can place a baking tray filled with water on the lower rack and place the small ramekin dishes into it.
- Turn the halogen oven to 150°C and cook for 40–45 minutes (20–30 minutes if you're using individual ramekin dishes). The pudding should have a golden sponge topping which is firm to touch.
- Serve with crème fraîche or Greek yoghurt. You will notice that the bottom half of the pudding is a gooey lemon sauce and the top should be a lovely light sponge.

50g butter
150g sugar
Zest and juice of 2 large or 3 medium lemons
4 medium eggs (or 3 large), separated
1 teaspoon vanilla essence or paste
50g plain flour
300ml milk
1 dessertspoon butter

SUITABLE FOR VEGETARIANS

SUITABLE FOR VEGETARIANS

# Chocolate, Apple and Hazelnut Betty

**SERVES 4–6**

3 Bramley cooking
  apples, cored,
  peeled and sliced
2 tablespoons sugar
1–2 tablespoons water
125g breadcrumbs
50g oats
50g hazelnuts,
  chopped
75g dark chocolate
  chunks (for a vegan
  version, use dairy-
  free chocolate)
2 teaspoons ground
  cinnamon
100g butter (for a
  vegan version, use
  dairy-free
  margarine)
3 tablespoons golden
  syrup

This is simply yummy!

- Preheat the halogen oven using the preheat setting or set the temperature to 190°C.
- Place the apple slices in an ovenproof dish. Sprinkle with the sugar and water. Then place on the low rack and cook for 10 minutes. Stir and cook for another 5 minutes before removing from the oven.
- Whilst the apples are cooking, combine the breadcrumbs, oats, hazelnuts, chocolate and cinnamon. Place this mixture over the top of the fruit.
- Place the butter and syrup in an ovenproof dish and melt using the heat from the halogen oven – do not allow it to burn. Once melted, pour this mixture over the crumble mixture.
- Return fruit betty to the halogen and place on the low rack. Cook for another 15–20 minutes until the top is golden.
- Serve with a dollop of crème fraîche or vanilla ice-cream.

SUITABLE FOR VEGETARIANS AND VEGANS

# Raspberry Healthy Brûlèe

SERVES 4–6

This is a really yummy dessert that takes minutes to prepare. I usually have frozen raspberries in my freezer and yoghurt and crème fraîche in my fridge. The brûlèe looks and tastes far more impressive than it really is and the good news is that it is actually quite healthy!

- I tend to prepare this dessert in the same heatproof dish I serve it in, which is large enough for 4–6 portions. Alternatively, you could use individual serving dishes such as ramekins – though make sure they are heatproof.
- If you have frozen raspberries, place them in your heatproof serving dish or other heatproof dish and put it on the high rack for 10 minutes with the halogen oven set to thaw.
- Meanwhile, mix the yoghurt and crème fraîche together in a bowl. Once combined, add the vanilla paste and stir well.
- Remove the raspberries from the halogen. If you are using a different serving dish, or ramekin dishes, place the raspberries in the bottom at this stage.
- Spoon over the yoghurt mixture and then a sprinkle of brown sugar – enough to form a generous layer to make the crème brûlèe effect.
- Place back in the halogen oven on the high rack. Turn to the highest setting (usually 250°C) for 3–4 minutes, allowing the brown sugar to start to melt and caramelise. The beauty of the halogen oven is that you can see the dessert cooking and therefore avoid it burning.
- Serve and enjoy!

SUITABLE FOR VEGETARIANS

200g frozen raspberries (or fresh)
350–400g Greek yoghurt (I use Total 0%)
3 tablespoons low-fat crème fraîche
1 teaspoon vanilla paste
3–4 tablespoons brown sugar

SERVES 4-6

115g sugar
115g butter
2 eggs, beaten
2 tablespoons milk
1 tablespoon vanilla
  essence or paste
100g self-raising flour
2 tablespoons cocoa
300ml boiling water
2 tablespoons sugar
1 tablespoon cocoa

# Chocolate Saucy Pudding

My mum used to make this when we were children and I rediscovered the recipe when I pinched her personal cookery notebook. We used to call this a magic pudding as the sauce is poured over the top of the cake, but during cooking it miraculously goes to the bottom. I have adapted it to suit the halogen and it works really well. You could make this in small ramekin dishes, but adjust the cooking time if you do so.

• Preheat the halogen oven using the preheat setting or set the temperature to 175°C.
• In your mixer, beat the sugar and butter together until creamy and fluffy. Gradually add the beaten eggs, milk and vanilla, and mix well before adding the flour and cocoa.
• Pour this sponge mixture into a greased ovenproof dish (or ramekin dishes) and smooth over until flat.
• In bowl or jug, mix the boiling water, sugar and cocoa together and stir thoroughly until dissolved and lump free. Pour this over the sponge mixture.
• Place on the low rack and cook for 40–50 minutes, until the sponge is firm to touch.
• Serve with a dollop of Greek yoghurt or crème fraîche and enjoy!

SUITABLE FOR VEGETARIANS

# Peach Melba Delight

This is another favourite in our house. It is similar to the Raspberry Healthy Brûlèe. You can use fresh peaches when they are in season or, if you are in a hurry, you could instead use tinned peaches in their own juice.

200g raspberries (frozen or fresh)
4–5 tablespoons brown sugar
350–400g Greek yoghurt
3 tablespoons low-fat crème fraîche
1 teaspoon vanilla paste
2–3 ripe peaches (or tinned peaches), sliced

- Place the frozen or fresh raspberries in an ovenproof dish and sprinkle with 1 tablespoon of sugar. Place on the low rack and cook for 5 minutes at 180°C to soften.
- Remove and crush. If you do not want the pips, you could put the raspberries through a sieve to form a finer purée rather than a mush.
- In a bowl, mix the yoghurt and crème fraîche together with the vanilla paste.
- Place the sliced peaches in the bottom of an ovenproof serving dish. Drizzle with two thirds of the raspberry purée.
- Add the raspberry purée to the crème fraîche mix and fold to create a ripple effect – don't over stir.
- Pour this onto the peaches and smooth to form an even coating. Cover with a generous covering of brown sugar.
- Place on the high rack for 3–4 minutes at 250°C. Watch it constantly, ensuring you are ready to remove it before it burns!
- Serve hot or cold.

SUITABLE FOR VEGETARIANS

# Apple and Cinnamon Cobbler

SERVES 4–6

Apple and cinnamon are a bit like strawberries and cream – they just fit together so well.

4–5 Bramley cooking apples
1–2 tablespoons brown sugar (depending on desired sweetness)
1–2 teaspoons ground cinnamon
Juice of ½ a lemon
50g raisins
30ml water
150g self-raising flour
25g sugar
50g butter
100ml natural yoghurt
1 teaspoon vanilla essence
Milk to brush
A little extra brown sugar to sprinkle

• Preheat the halogen oven using the preheat setting or set the temperature to 200°C.
• Place the apples, brown sugar, cinnamon, lemon juice and raisins in a saucepan. Add the water. Cook on a medium heat until the apples start to soften, but not completely – you still want them to have some firmness.
• Meanwhile, sift the flour and place it with the sugar in a bowl. Rub the butter into the flour until it resembles breadcrumbs. Add the yoghurt and vanilla essence and mix.
• Place on a floured surface and roll into a thick sausage. Then cut into 4–5cm pieces.
• Pour the apple mixture into an ovenproof or casserole dish, first making sure it fits well in your halogen oven. Place the scones around the edge and top of the apple mixture. Coat with a little milk and a sprinkle of brown sugar.
• Place on the low rack and cook for 15–18 minutes until the scones are golden.

SUITABLE FOR VEGETARIANS

# Queen of Puddings

My mum used to make this for us when we were children. Comforting puddings are making a well-earned revival – they're so much nicer than shop-bought, processed puddings.

- Preheat the halogen oven using the preheat setting or set the temperature to 180°C.
- Grease an ovenproof dish.
- Place the cubed bread in a bowl and sprinkle with the sugar.
- Heat the milk, vanilla extract and butter to almost boiling point and then pour over the bread and sugar mixture. When cool, add the egg yolks and whisk until smooth.
- Pour this into the greased ovenproof dish. Place on the low rack and cook for 30–35 minutes until set.
- Whilst this is cooking, beat the egg whites until they form soft peaks, gradually adding ½ of the caster sugar.
- Melt the jam on low heat as you don't want to burn it.
- Spread the jam over the set mixture. Top it with the whisked egg whites and sprinkle with the remaining caster sugar.
- Place back in the oven and cook for another 8–10 minutes until golden.

SUITABLE FOR VEGETARIANS

SERVES 4–6

90g white bread, cubed
45g sugar
420ml milk
1 teaspoon vanilla extract or paste
45g butter
2 eggs, separated
60g caster sugar
3 tablespoons jam (I use raspberry but feel free to use whatever you prefer)

SERVES 4–6

750g plums, halved,
   with stones removed
1–2 tablespoons runny
   honey
75g sugar
100ml Pink Port
50ml water
Icing sugar to sprinkle
Amaretti biscuits to
   serve

# Boozy Plums

A perfect dinner party dessert – make it as boozy as you like,
but off set the alcoholic taste with some creamy vanilla ice-
cream or cream.

• Preheat the halogen oven using the preheat setting or
  set the temperature to 150°C.
• Place the halved and stoned plums on a non-stick
  baking tray or ovenproof dish.
• Drizzle over the honey and sprinkle with a little sugar.
  Add the port and water before placing on the low
  rack and cooking for 30–40 minutes until the plums
  are soft.
• Remove and serve in individual bowls. Sprinkle with
  icing sugar and serve with some Amaretti biscuits.

SUITABLE FOR VEGETARIANS

# Apple and Date Bread and Butter Pudding

*A twist to a traditional favourite.*

- Grease an ovenproof dish with butter. Butter the bread slices and line the dish, sprinkling dates, apple, sugar and cinnamon between the slices.
- In a jug, mix the eggs, milk and cream (if used) together. Pour this over the bread mixture, pushing the bread down into the liquid where necessary. I then let this sit for about 10 minutes to absorb the milk.
- Preheat the halogen oven using the preheat setting or set the temperature to 190°C.
- Push down the bread into the liquid, sprinkle with more cinnamon if you like the flavour and place the dish on the low rack of the halogen.
- Cook for 30 minutes until the top is golden and the base is almost set.

SUITABLE FOR VEGETARIANS

**SERVES 4–6**

4–6 slices of white
  bread (stale is ideal)
30g butter
40g dates, chopped
1 cooking apple,
  peeled and chopped
50g sugar
2 teaspoons ground
  cinnamon
2 eggs, beaten
300ml milk
75ml cream (optional
  – instead you can
  increase the quantity
  of milk to 375ml and
  remember that
  whole milk is
  creamier)

# French Apple Tart

SERVES 4–6

150g plain flour
75g butter
75g sugar
1 egg, beaten
1 tablespoon water
1kg cooking apples
Squeeze of lemon
  juice
15g butter
60g sugar
1–2 teaspoons ground
  cinnamon
3 tablespoons apricot
  jam

This is a lovely dish. The recipe includes the process for making the pastry case but, if you aren't up to making your own, you could buy readymade sweet pastry or ready-cooked pastry cases, but they will obviously be more expensive than making your own.

- To make the pastry, place the flour in a bowl. Add the butter and rub to form a texture similar to breadcrumbs. Add the sugar and combine well. Add the beaten egg and water and combine to form a dough. Then place the dough in the fridge to rest while you continue with the rest of the recipe.
- Peel and thinly slice the apples and cover them with water and a squeeze of lemon juice.
- Preheat the halogen oven using the preheat setting or set the temperature to 200°C.
- Roll out the pastry and line a flan dish, first making sure it fits in the halogen oven. Prick the pastry with a fork and place on the low rack of the oven for 15 minutes to bake blind. Cover the pastry with baking beans placed over a sheet of baking parchment if you want to prevent air bubbles forming in the pastry.
- Whilst that is cooking, remove a third of the apple slices and place them in a pan to soften with a little butter, a drizzle of water and 1 dessertspoon of sugar. Stir until soft before adding almost all the cinnamon.

- Remove the pastry case and smooth on the puréed apple. Over the top of this, place the apple slices in a nice even pattern, fanning out and overlapping slightly around the flan dish. Sprinkle with sugar and the remaining cinnamon.
- Return to the low rack and bake for 25 minutes until the apples are cooked. Remove from the oven.
- Gently heat the apricot jam, stirring continuously to avoid burning. Once the jam is runny, brush it over the baked apple ensuring the top is well covered.
- Serve hot or cold with ice-cream, cream fraîche or just on its own.

SUITABLE FOR VEGETARIANS

# Pineapple Upside Down Cake

SERVES 4–6

150g butter
150g sugar
3 eggs, beaten
150g self-raising flour,
    sifted
1 teaspoon vanilla
    essence
50g butter
50g brown sugar
2 tablespoons golden
    syrup
6 pineapple rings
3 glace cherries,
    halved
Crème fraîche to serve

A traditional family favourite that can be used as a pudding or a cake.

- In your food mixer, mix 150g of butter and 150g of sugar until golden and creamy.
- Gradually add the eggs and combine well.
- Fold in the sifted flour and, once combined thoroughly, add the vanilla essence.
- Preheat the halogen oven using the preheat setting or set the temperature to 180°C.
- Place 50g of butter, the brown sugar and golden syrup in an ovenproof bowl and, using the preheat temperature, melt the butter, but do not let it burn.
- Grease or line an ovenproof dish or cake tin thoroughly.
- Place a small amount of the butter and sugar mixture into the dish and then place the pineapples in the bottom with the cherries in the middle of the pineapple rings. Pour on the remaining melted butter and sugar.
- Carefully spoon on the sponge mix to cover the pineapple rings. Once completely covered, carefully smooth over the surface.
- Place on the low rack and cook until the sponge has risen, is golden and springs back into shape when touched – this should take between 25 and 30 minutes.
- Remove from the oven. Place a plate or serving dish over the top of the cake dish and flip over so that the cake sits on the plate, upside down, pineapple facing upwards.
- Serve with a dollop of crème fraîche.

SUITABLE FOR VEGETARIANS

# Rhubarb and Strawberry Crumbly

This is a lovely pudding, with a light crumbly topping. You can use other fruit combinations to create your own version, but this is our favourite.

- Preheat the halogen oven using the preheat setting or set the temperature to 180°C.
- Place the prepared fruit in the bottom of an ovenproof dish. Sprinkle with the sugar and add the water.
- Place on the low rack and cook for 15 minutes to soften the fruit.
- Whilst this is cooking, crumble the biscuits using a food processor or place the biscuits in a bag and bash gently but firmly with the end of a rolling pin to form crumbs.
- Remove the fruit from the oven. Stir well before sprinkling the biscuit crumbs over the top to form a crumble topping. Place this back in the oven and cook for another 15 minutes.
- Serve with a dollop of crème fraîche or vanilla ice-cream.

SUITABLE FOR VEGETARIANS

SERVES 4–6

350g rhubarb, sliced
150g strawberries, halved (or use frozen if not in season)
1–2 tablespoons of sugar (depending on preferred sweetness)
2 tablespoons water
½ packet of biscuits (I use digestives or oaty biscuits)

# Fruit Berry Betty

2–3 Bramley cooking
  apples, cored,
  peeled and sliced
300g mixed frozen
  berries
1–2 tablespoons sugar
1–2 tablespoons water
125g breadcrumbs
50g oats
2 teaspoons cinnamon
  powder
100g butter (for the
  vegan version, use
  dairy-free
  margarine)
3 tablespoons golden
  syrup

Fill this wonderful pudding with a mixture of fruit and berries for a great burst of vitamin C, zing and taste sensation. A great variation to the standard fruit crumble.

- Preheat the halogen oven using the preheat setting or set the temperature to 190°C.
- Place the apple and berries in an ovenproof dish. Sprinkle with the sugar and water. Place on the low rack and cook for 10 minutes. Stir and cook for another 5 minutes before removing from the oven.
- Whilst the apple and berries are cooking, combine the breadcrumbs, oats and cinnamon. Place this mixture over the top of the fruit.
- Place the butter and syrup in an ovenproof dish and melt using the heat from the halogen oven – do not allow it to burn. Once melted, pour this mixture over the crumble mixture.
- Return fruit betty to the halogen and place on the low rack. Cook for another 15–20 minutes until the top is golden.
- Serve with a dollop of crème fraîche or vanilla ice-cream.

SUITABLE FOR VEGETARIANS AND VEGANS

# Roasted Plums

SERVES 4–6

It is not just vegetables that can be roasted, plums are delicious when slow cooked and they are perfect for the halogen.

8–12 plums
Sugar
2–3 tablespoons water
1–2 tablespoons of
   honey
Ground cinnamon

- Preheat the halogen oven using the preheat setting or set the temperature to 180°C.
- Wash the plums. While they are still wet roll them in sugar and place on a greased or buttered baking tray or ovenproof dish. Add the water.
- Place on the low rack and cook for 10 minutes.
- Drizzle honey over the plums and sprinkle with cinnamon before cooking again for another 10–15 minutes until they are cooked.
- Serve with custard, crème fraîche or ice-cream.

SUITABLE FOR VEGETARIANS

# Apple and Blackberry Frangipane Tart

150g plain flour
75g butter
75g sugar
1 egg, beaten
1 tablespoon water
125g butter
125g sugar
2 eggs
125g ground almonds
1 tablespoon plain
flour
1–2 teaspoons ground
cinnamon
2 apples, sliced
40g blackberries
2 tablespoons apricot
jam

I love the look of this tart almost as much as the taste. Sprinkle with icing sugar before serving. Delicious hot or cold.

- To make the pastry, place the flour in a bowl. Add the butter and rub to form a texture similar to breadcrumbs. Add the sugar and combine well. Add the beaten egg and water and combine to form a dough. Then place the dough in the fridge to rest while you continue with the rest of the recipe.
- Preheat the halogen oven using the preheat setting or set the temperature to 200°C.
- Roll out the pastry and line a flan dish, first making sure it fits in the halogen. Prick the pastry with a fork and place on the low rack of the oven for 15 minutes to bake blind. Cover the pastry with baking beans placed over a sheet of baking parchment if you want to prevent air bubbles forming in the pastry.
- Whilst the pastry is cooking, beat the butter and sugar together until light and fluffy. Gradually add the eggs. When this is well beaten, add the ground almonds, flour and cinnamon. Beat well.
- Pour this mixture onto the pastry case. Over the top, place the apple slices in a nice even pattern around the flan dish. Add the blackberries in between the apple slices and press into the sponge mixture.
- Return to the low rack and bake for 25–30 minutes until the apples are cooked and the sponge has risen. Remove from the oven.

- Gently heat the apricot jam, stirring continuously to avoid it burning. Once the jam is runny, brush it over the baked apples ensuring the top is well covered and to form a glaze. Return the tart to the halogen for 5 more minutes.
- Serve hot or cold with ice-cream, cream fraîche or just on its own.

SUITABLE FOR VEGETARIANS

# Cheat's Ginger and Apple Layer

SERVES 4–6

700g Bramley apples, cored, peeled and diced
2 tablespoons water
50g brown sugar
50g sultanas
1 teaspoon ground cinnamon
1 small ginger cake, crumbled
Juice and zest of 1 orange
1 tablespoon desiccated coconut
1 tablespoon brown sugar

This is such a simple dish using some store-cupboard staples. It can be thrown together in minutes – perfect for a quick and easy dessert.

- Place the chopped apple in a saucepan with the water and sugar. Cook until it starts to soften, but still has a bite (i.e. don't purée it). Add the sultanas and cinnamon and combine well.
- Preheat the halogen oven using the preheat setting or set the temperature to 180°C.
- Grease an ovenproof dish.
- Crumble a layer of ginger cake in the bottom of the ovenproof dish. Over this, add a layer of apple. Repeat, finishing with a ginger cake top layer.
- Pour over the orange juice and zest. Sprinkle with the coconut and 1 tablespoon of brown sugar.
- Place on the low rack and cook for 15–20 minutes.
- Serve with homemade custard or Butterscotch Sauce (see the next recipe) … delicious!

SUITABLE FOR VEGETARIANS

# Butterscotch Sauce

- Place the butter, brown sugar and golden syrup in an ovenproof bowl (or saucepan if you prefer not to use the halogen oven). Melt together gently but don't let it burn. Stir well to combine.
- Fold in double cream (it must be double cream as single may curdle or separate).
- Serve hot or cold.

SUITABLE FOR VEGETARIANS

60g butter
120g brown sugar
6 tablespoons golden
  syrup
6 tablespoons double
  cream

# Homemade Custard

600ml full fat milk
4 egg yolks
4 tablespoons
  cornflour
3 tablespoons sugar
1 teaspoon vanilla
  essence

- Heat the milk until just below boiling point. While it is heating, mix the egg yolks, cornflour and sugar together. Be careful to keep an eye on the milk to avoid it spilling over.
- Remove the milk from the heat and add the egg mixture. Use a hand whisk and stir well.
- Place back on the heat and continue to stir until the custard starts to thicken – be careful not to have the heat too high or it will burn.
- Once the custard has reached your desired thickness, remove it from the heat. Serve immediately.

*Note:* If you have any custard left over, you could pour it into lolly moulds and freeze – these make delicious ice-lollies!

SUITABLE FOR VEGETARIANS

# Pear and Dark Chocolate Granola Layer

You can mix granola with dark chocolate chips, or try Dorset Cereals' amazing dark chocolate granola cereals – though I must warn you, they are seriously addictive! This pudding is lovely hot or cold.

- Place the pears in a saucepan with the water and cook until they start to soften. Once softened, stir in the sugar.
- Preheat the halogen oven using the preheat setting or set the temperature to 180°C.
- Mix the granola, chocolate chips and hazelnuts together.
- Spoon half the pears into an ovenproof dish. Cover with a layer of granola mix. Add the final layer of pears and cover again with the granola mixture.
- Place in the oven on the low rack and cook for 15 minutes.
- Serve hot or cold.

SUITABLE FOR VEGETARIANS

8 ripe pears, peeled, cored, and diced
2 tablespoons water
1 tablespoon sugar
8–12 tablespoons granola
75g dark chocolate chips (if you are not using dark chocolate granola)
2 tablespoons hazelnuts, chopped

# Cakes and Treats

Most people worry about using the halogen oven to bake cakes. Many believe that their cake will burn on top and remain uncooked in the middle, but don't panic, this only happens if you have the temperature too high. Remember, the halogen oven comes with a powerful fan that helps distribute the heat around the bowl evenly.

# Chocolate Chip Cupcakes with Vanilla Butter Icing

**MAKES 8–12**

50g cocoa
15ml boiling water
175g butter
175g sugar
3 eggs, beaten
175g self-raising flour
50g plain chocolate
   chips

**Vanilla Butter Icing:**
50g butter
100g cream cheese
200–275g icing sugar
1 teaspoon vanilla
   essence or paste
Chocolate chips or
   grated chocolate to
   sprinkle

- Preheat the halogen oven using the preheat setting or set to 200°C.
- Mix the cocoa with the hot water and leave to one side.
- Cream the butter and sugar together until pale and fluffy. Add the eggs a little at a time and continue to beat well.
- Sift the flour and fold into the mixture gently.
- When thoroughly mixed, add the cocoa mixture and chocolate chips and combine.
- Place in cupcake or muffin cases in a muffin or cupcake tray. I have not been able to find a round muffin tray so I use silicon muffin cases and place them on the halogen baking trays that come with the accessory packs. You can comfortably fit 10 on the tray. This recipe should make 8–12 cakes depending on their size.
- Place on the low rack and cook for 12–15 minutes. The cakes should be firm and spring back when touched. Once cooked, place them on a cooling rack to cool.
- While the cakes are cooling, prepare the icing. Beat the butter and cream cheese together until soft. Gradually add the icing sugar and vanilla essence and beat until you reach the desired consistency – it should be glossy, thick and lump free. The best way of testing to see if you have added enough icing sugar is to taste it. It should taste sweet and creamy but not too buttery.

- If you are using silicon muffin cases, wait until the cakes are cool, then carefully pull away at the sides of each case. Once the case is clear all the way around, turn it upside down and the cake should pop out.
- Place the icing into an icing bag and fold down the ends to secure. Start in the centre of the cake and spiral outwards covering the whole of the cake top, gently overlapping to avoid gaps. Finish with a sprinkle of a few chocolate chips or grated chocolate and you are ready to serve.

SUITABLE FOR VEGETARIANS

# Fruit Scones

MAKES 8–10

200g self-raising flour
30g butter
30g sugar
50g raisins or mixed
  fruit
125ml milk

- Preheat the halogen oven to 210°C.
- Sift the flour into a bowl. Add the butter and rub to form breadcrumbs. Add the sugar and dried fruit and combine well.
- Gradually add the milk to form a dough which is firm but not wet.
- Place the dough on a floured board and press out to reach a 3–4cm thickness. Cut out the scones with a pastry cutter and place on a greased baking tray. Brush with milk.
- Place in the halogen oven on the low rack for 10–12 minutes.
- When cooked, place on a cooling rack. Serve with cream and jam for a traditional cream tea.

SUITABLE FOR VEGETARIANS

# Boiled Fruit and Tea Loaf

This is an old recipe, which I have slightly adapted. It is really easy to make.

- Put the kettle on and make 200ml of tea (without milk!) and leave it to stew for 5 minutes.
- Meanwhile, in a large saucepan add the dried fruit, butter and sugar. Then add the tea when it's ready.
- Place on a moderate heat and gently allow the butter to melt and the sugar to dissolve. Keep stirring as you don't want this to stick or burn. Once it is melted, add the spices. Boil for 1 minute, then remove from the heat.
- Using sharp scissors, snip the apple rings into pieces and drop them into the saucepan. Stir well and leave until cold, or overnight if you prefer.
- Once the tea mixture has cooled and been absorbed, sift in the flour and stir well until thoroughly combined.
- Preheat the halogen oven using the preheat setting or set the temperature to 180°C.
- Thoroughly grease or line a loaf tin and pour in the mixture. (I use cake liners as they are easy and worry free.)
- Place on the low rack and cook for 20 minutes. Check the cake and, if the top is getting too dark, cover with some brown paper – but make sure it is secure without restricting the cake.
- Turn the temperature down to 160°C and cook for another 25–30 minutes, or until a skewer, when inserted into the centre of the cake, comes out clean.
- Leave the loaf to cool in the cake tin before turning it out onto a cooling rack.

**MAKES APPROXIMATELY 8 SLICES**

220ml stewed tea
300g mixed dried fruit
125g butter (for the vegan version, use dairy-free margarine)
125g brown sugar
2 teaspoons ground cinnamon
1 teaspoon allspice
40g dried apple rings
225g self-raising flour

SUITABLE FOR VEGETARIANS AND VEGANS

175g butter
150g sugar
3 large eggs, beaten
175g self-raising flour
125g sultanas
2 tablespoons lemon
    curd
Juice and zest of 1
    lemon for topping
100g sugar for topping

SUITABLE FOR VEGETARIANS

# Mum's Lemon Curd Cupcakes

This is one of my mum's favourite recipes. The cupcakes are ideal for packed lunches but, beware, they might not last that long – they are yummy eaten warm!

- Preheat the halogen oven using the preheat setting or set the temperature to 200°C.
- Cream the butter and sugar together until pale and fluffy. Add the eggs a little at a time and continue to beat well.
- Sift the flour and fold into the mixture gently. When thoroughly mixed, roughly fold in the sultanas and lemon curd. Don't over fold, as you want the lemon curd to have a ripple effect.
- Place the mixture in cupcake or muffin cases in a muffin or cupcake tray. I have not been able to find a round muffin tray, so I use silicon muffin cases and place them on the halogen baking trays that come with the accessory packs. You can comfortably fit 10 on the tray. This recipe should make 8–12 cakes depending on their size.
- Place on the low rack and cook for 12–15 minutes. The cakes should be firm and spring back when touched.
- While the cakes are cooking, juice and zest 1 lemon. Then mix the juice and zest together. Once the cakes are cooked and still hot, pour a little of the lemon mix over each one and finish with a sprinkle of sugar.
- If you are using silicon muffin cases, wait until the cakes are cool, then carefully pull away at the sides of each case. Once the case is clear all the way around, turn it upside down and the cake should pop out.

# Cappuccino Cupcakes

MAKES 8–12

- Preheat the halogen oven using the preheat setting or set the temperature to 200°C.
- Cream the butter and sugar together until pale and fluffy. Add the eggs a little at a time and continue to beat well.
- Sift the flour and fold into the mixture gently. When thoroughly mixed, add the coffee essence and combine.
- Place the mixture in cupcake or muffin cases in a muffin or cupcake tray. I use silicon muffin cases and place them on the halogen baking trays that come with the accessory packs. You can comfortably fit 10 on the tray.
- Place on the low rack and cook for 12–15 minutes. The cakes should be firm and spring back when touched.
- While the cakes are cooling, prepare the icing. Beat the butter and cream cheese together until soft. Gradually add the icing sugar and vanilla essence and beat until you reach the desired consistency – it should be glossy, thick and lump free. The best way of testing to see if you have added enough icing sugar is to taste it. It should taste sweet and creamy but not too buttery.
- If you are using silicon muffin cases, wait until the cakes are cool, then carefully pull away at the sides of each case. Once the case is clear all the way around, turn it upside down and the cake should pop out.
- Place the icing into an icing bag and fold down the ends to secure. Start in the centre of the cake and spiral outwards covering the whole of the cake top, gently overlapping to avoid gaps. Finish with a sprinkle with cocoa to give a cappuccino effect, and you are ready to serve.

175g butter
175g sugar
3 eggs, beaten
175g self-raising flour
2–4 teaspoons coffee essence, depending on desired strength

**Vanilla Butter Icing:**
50g butter
100g cream cheese
200–275g icing sugar
1 teaspoon vanilla essence or paste
Cocoa to sprinkle

SUITABLE FOR VEGETARIANS

175g butter
175g sugar
3 eggs, beaten
200g self-raising flour
Juice and zest of 2
   lemons

**Icing:**
50g butter
100g cream cheese
300g icing sugar
Zest of 1 lemon
Slices of lemon to
   garnish

# Lemon Cream Sponge

This is a lovely sponge with a lemon creamy filling. If you prefer, you can also put the lemon cream all over the cake for a really decadent gâteau.

• Preheat the halogen oven using the preheat setting or set the temperature to 180°C.
• Cream the butter and sugar together until pale and fluffy. Add the eggs a little at a time and continue to beat well.
• Sift the flour and fold into the mixture gently. When thoroughly mixed, add the juice and zest of the lemons and combine. For an extra lemon tang you could add a little lemon essence, but buy a good quality one or it can taste too artificial.
• Place the mixture in 2 greased sponge tins.
• Turn the halogen oven down to 160°C, with the fan on full (if applicable).
• If you have an extension ring, you could cook the sponges together. If you don't, I would advise cooking them on the low rack one at a time. If you use an extension ring, place one sponge on the low rack and one on the high rack but keep an eye on the top one. You may want to swap them over halfway through cooking or the top sponge may be ready a few minutes before the lower one.
• Bake for 25–35 minutes until firm to the touch and the sponge has pulled away slightly from the edges of the tin.

- While the sponges are cooling, prepare the icing. Beat the butter and cream cheese together until soft. Gradually add the icing sugar and vanilla essence and beat until you reach the desired consistency – it should be glossy, thick and lump free. The best way of testing to see if you have added enough icing sugar is to taste it. It should taste sweet and creamy but not too buttery.

- Spread the icing on one of the sponges and then sandwich them both together. For an extra touch of lemon, you could spread with lemon curd and then spread on the butter icing before sandwiching together. If you prefer, you can place icing on the top or around the sides, or even all over. Finish with a couple of slices of lemon to garnish.

SUITABLE FOR VEGETARIANS

# Blueberry Muffins

MAKES 8–12

175g golden sugar
2 eggs, beaten
250ml natural yoghurt
1 teaspoon vanilla
  extract
300g self-raising flour
175g blueberries

- Preheat the halogen oven using the preheat setting or set the temperature to 190°C.
- Beat the sugar and eggs together until fluffy. Add the yoghurt and vanilla extract and beat again.
- Sift the flour into the mixture and carefully fold into the mix. When thoroughly mixed, add the blueberries.
- Place the mixture in cupcake or muffin cases in a muffin or cupcake tray. I have not been able to find a round muffin tray, so I use silicon muffin cases and place them on the halogen baking trays that come with the accessory packs. You can comfortably fit 10 on the tray. This recipe should make 8–12 cakes depending on their size.
- Place on the low rack and cook for 12–15 minutes. The cakes should be firm and spring back when touched.
- Place onto a cooling rack before serving.

SUITABLE FOR VEGETARIANS

# Upside Down Blackberry and Apple Cake

A spring, loose-bottomed cake tin is ideal for baking this cake.

2–3 cooking apples, sliced
150g blackberries
1 tablespoon sugar
175g butter
175g sugar
3 eggs
175g self-raising flour
1 teaspoon vanilla extract
2 teaspoons ground cinnamon
Icing sugar to serve

- Preheat the halogen oven using the preheat setting or set the temperature to 190°C.
- Generously grease a cake tin with butter.
- Place the apple slices, blackberries and 1 tablespoon of sugar in the base of the cake tin.
- Beat the butter and sugar until light and fluffy. Add the eggs a little at a time, and then add the sifted flour. Once mixed, add the vanilla extract and cinnamon. Combine well.
- Place the cake mixture over the apple and blackberries. Smooth the surface gently.
- Place on the low rack and cook for 30–40 minutes, until the cake is cooked, firm and springs back to shape when touched.
- When you are ready to serve, place an upturned plate on the top of the cake tin. Flip it over so that the cake tin is upside down on top of the plate, and then allow the cake to drop down onto the plate. If you are using a spring cake tin, undo it to release the cake.
- Sprinkle with sifted icing sugar to decorate before serving hot or cold.

SUITABLE FOR VEGETARIANS

# Aunty Ruth's Fabulous Dark Ginger Cake

When I was growing up, a visit to Aunty Ruth's house meant afternoon tea with delicious cakes and jelly and blancmange in the shape of rabbits. Here is one of her great recipes – I hope you enjoy it.

**MAKES APPROXIMATELY 8 PIECES**

½ teaspoon bicarbonate of soda
4 tablespoons milk
125g butter
125g moist brown sugar
185g black treacle or golden syrup
250g plain flour
10g ground ginger
1 teaspoon grated lemon rind
1 egg
Candied ginger to serve

- Preheat the halogen oven using the preheat setting or set the temperature to 150°C.
- Blend the bicarbonate of soda with 1 tablespoon of milk.
- Put the butter, sugar and syrup in a saucepan and heat until the butter has melted. Add the milk and heat gently.
- Sieve the flour and ginger together in a bowl. Add the melted butter and syrup mixture, along with the milk and bicarbonate mixture, lemon rind and egg. Whisk until well combined.
- Thoroughly grease or line a cake tin (I use a 7 inch (18cm) tin). Pour in the mixture and bake on the low rack for 1 hour, 10 minutes, to 1 hour, 30 minutes. To test to see if it is cooked, gently press the centre of the cake – if there is no impression it is cooked.
- Leave the cake in the tin until cool and then turn onto a cooling rack.
- Serve iced or topped with sliced candied ginger.

SUITABLE FOR VEGETARIANS

# Chocolate and Date Fingers

This is a lovely, chocolaty, flapjack-style snack and it is very addictive. All you need is a lovely cup of tea, a good book and a comfy sofa – life cannot get any better!

- Preheat the halogen oven using the preheat setting or set the temperature to 175°C.
- In a saucepan, melt the chocolate, butter, sugar and syrup on a low/medium heat, making sure it does not burn. Stir continuously.
- Add the chopped dates and the oats. Mix well.
- Pour into a greased tin or ovenproof dish. Press down gently.
- Place on the low rack and cook for 20–25 minutes.
- Leave in the tin to cool. Once cooled, cut into fingers.

SUITABLE FOR VEGETARIANS AND VEGANS

60g plain cooking chocolate (for the vegan version, use dairy-free chocolate)
185g butter (for the vegan version, use dairy-free margarine)
60g brown sugar
1 tablespoon golden syrup
125g dates, roughly chopped
250g oats

MAKES 4–6

½ pack of puff pastry
½ small jar of
  mincemeat
25g melted butter
Sprinkling of brown
  sugar

# Simple Cheating Eccles Cakes

These were my dad's favourite when I was growing up. Funny, I never really liked them when I was a child – a bit like Garibaldi biscuits … we thought they were packed with dead flies! I have matured since then and found I really love them. They don't last long in our home, so here is a very fast and easy recipe to suit the craving.

- Preheat the halogen oven using the preheat setting or turn the temperature to 200°C.
- Roll out the puff pastry to about 4–5mm thick. Cut into squares, approximately 6–8 inches square.
- Place 2–3 teaspoons of mincemeat in the centre of each puff pastry square.
- Using a pastry brush, brush melted butter around the edges of the square. I normally fold the pastry diagonally, bringing each corner to the centre to form an envelope or parcel. Alternatively, you can simply fold the pastry over and secure, either to form a rectangle or a triangle.
- On a floured surface, turn the cakes over so that the seam is on the bottom. Apply a bit of pressure on your rolling pin, or use your fingers, and gently roll the cakes flat, being careful not to split the pastry.
- Using a sharp knife, score 2 or 3 slits in the top of the cakes. Brush with butter and sprinkle with brown sugar before placing on a greased baking tray.
- Place on the low rack and bake for 15–18 minutes until golden.

SUITABLE FOR VEGETARIANS

# Jam Turnovers

MAKES 4–6

If I am making some Eccles cakes, my youngest son usually demands to help and inevitably wants to make Jam Turnovers. The recipe is similar to the Eccles recipe above, so I would suggest combining both to save time and money!

½ pack of puff pastry
Jam of your choice
A little milk or beaten egg
A little butter, melted
Brown sugar to sprinkle

- Preheat the halogen oven using the preheat setting or turn the temperature to 200°C.
- Roll out the puff pastry to about 4–5mm thick. Cut into squares, approximately 6–8 inches square.
- Place 2–3 teaspoons of jam in the centre of each puff pastry square.
- Using a pastry brush, brush milk or egg around the edges of the square. I normally fold the pastry diagonally to form a triangle. Secure the edges by crimping.
- Brush with butter and a sprinkle of brown sugar before placing on a greased baking tray.
- Place on the low rack and bake for 15–18 minutes until golden.

SUITABLE FOR VEGETARIANS

# Apple Turnovers

**SERVES 4–6**

½ pack of puff pastry

Stewed apple or 2 cooking apples, cut into fine slices

Beaten egg or milk

Brown sugar to sprinkle

Ground cinnamon to taste (optional)

These are great if you have any spare puff pastry or stewed apple to use up. Stewed apple is easiest, but you can also simply slice some cooking apples into the centre of the pastry, add some sugar and off you go.

- Preheat the halogen oven using the preheat setting or set the temperature to 200°C.
- Roll out the puff pastry to about 4–5mm thick. Cut into squares, approximately 6–8 inches square.
- Place 2–3 teaspoons of stewed apple or apple slices in the centre of the puff pastry squares. If you are using apple slices, add a sprinkle of sugar and cinnamon to taste.
- Using a pastry brush, brush the milk or egg around the edges of the square. I normally fold the pastry diagonally to form a triangle. Secure the edges by crimping.
- Brush with butter and a sprinkle of brown sugar before placing on a greased baking tray.
- Place on the low rack and bake for 15–18 minutes until golden.

SUITABLE FOR VEGETARIANS

# Banana and Chocolate Cake

- Preheat the halogen oven using the preheat setting or set the temperature to 190°C.
- Using a cake mixer, beat the sugar and butter together until light and fluffy. Add the honey, vanilla essence and beaten eggs and mix again.
- Add the banana, before adding the sifted flour and cocoa. Combine well.
- Pour into a well greased or lined cake or loaf tin and bake on the low rack for 30 minutes, or until a skewer comes out clean when pushed into the centre of the cake.
- Remove from the halogen and leave to cool slightly before turning out onto a cooling rack.
- Decorate with melted chocolate or vanilla butter icing (see the Cupcake recipes for the recipe).

SUITABLE FOR VEGETARIANS

125g sugar
125g butter
2 tablespoons honey
1 teaspoon vanilla
  essence
2 eggs, beaten
1 ripe banana, mashed
150g self-raising flour
4 tablespoons cocoa

50g butter
75g oats
30g brown sugar
30g plain flour
75g sugar
1 egg, beaten
2 tablespoons natural
    yoghurt
1 teaspoon vanilla
    essence
50g self-raising flour
100g chopped dates
50g chopped walnuts
Extra brown sugar to
    sprinkle

# Date and Walnut Slice

This is a really nice and healthy alternative to a cake. For added indulgence, you could add a handful of plain chocolate chips to the mixture.

- Heat the butter in a saucepan or in a bowl in the halogen oven (making sure it doesn't burn). Once melted, remove from heat and stir in the oats, brown sugar and flour.
- Press into a lined baking tray to form the base of the slices.
- Preheat the halogen oven using the preheat setting or set the temperature to 180°C.
- While the oven is heating, beat the sugar and egg together. Once light and fluffy, add the yoghurt and vanilla essence.
- Add the flour, dates and most of the walnuts, retaining a few to use on the top of the slices. Pour this mixture on top of the base. Spread it to cover the base and sprinkle with the remaining walnuts and a little brown sugar.
- Place on the low rack and cook for 20 minutes.
- Leave to cool for 5–10 minutes before slicing.

SUITABLE FOR VEGETARIANS

# Viennese Whirls

MAKES 18–22 BISCUITS

When I was a teenager, my mum and I used to catch a bus to Exeter to go shopping for clothes and generally spend a girlie day together. On the way home we would always buy a pack of M&S Viennese Whirls and, before we arrived home, the pack would be empty. Not much has changed since then; I can still demolish a whole portion of these delicious biscuits! This is a recipe where you really do need to use good quality butter as margarine does not really give the same taste or result.

200g butter
50g icing sugar
½ teaspoon vanilla
   paste
150g plain flour, sifted
50g cornflour, sifted

- Preheat the halogen oven using the preheat setting or set the temperature to 200°C.
- Beat the butter, icing sugar and vanilla paste together until light and fluffy.
- Gradually add the sifted flour and cornflour until you have a firm but squeezable paste.
- Pop this into your piping bag to create lovely swirly biscuits or, if you don't want to mess around with piping bags, you can carefully spoon dollops onto a greased baking tray. Make sure this tray fits well in your halogen oven – you will probably have enough mixture for two batches.
- Place on the low rack. (If you have an extension ring, you could bake both batches at the same time but watch the top layer, as they will cook faster than the bottom layer!) Bake for 10–15 minutes until golden.
- Place on a cooling rack before enjoying. Store in an airtight container once cooled.

SUITABLE FOR VEGETARIANS

# Carrot Cake Muffins with Vanilla Butter Icing

175g butter
175g brown sugar
3 eggs, beaten
175g self-raising flour
2 teaspoons cinnamon
    powder
1 teaspoon ground
    coriander
2 carrots, grated
50g desiccated
    coconut

**Vanilla Butter Icing:**
50g butter
100g cream cheese
200–275g icing sugar
1 teaspoon vanilla
    essence or paste

- Preheat the halogen oven using the preheat setting or set the temperature to 200°C.
- Cream the butter and sugar together until pale and fluffy. Add the eggs a little at a time and continue to beat well. Sift the flour and fold into the mixture gently.
- When thoroughly mixed, add the cinnamon, coriander, carrots and coconut. Combine well.
- Place the mixture in cupcake or muffin cases in a muffin or cupcake tray. I have not been able to find a round muffin tray, so I use silicon muffin cases and place them on the halogen baking trays that come with the accessory packs. You can comfortably fit 10 on the tray. This recipe should make 8–12 cakes depending on their size.
- Place on the low rack and cook for 15–18 minutes. The cakes should be firm and spring back when touched. Place on a cooling rack to cool.
- While the cakes are cooling, prepare the icing. Beat the butter and cream cheese together until soft. Gradually add the icing sugar and vanilla essence and beat until you reach the desired consistency – it should be glossy, thick and lump free. The best way of testing to see if you have added enough icing sugar is to taste it. It should taste sweet and creamy but not too buttery.

- If you are using silicon muffin cases, wait until the cakes are cool, then carefully pull away at the sides of each case. Once the case is clear all the way around, turn it upside down and the cake should pop out.
- Place the icing into an icing bag and fold down the ends to secure. Start in the centre of each cooled cake and spiral outwards covering the whole of the cake top, gently overlapping to avoid gaps.

SUITABLE FOR VEGETARIANS

# Breakfast Muffins

110g butter
110g brown sugar
2 eggs, beaten
110g self-raising flour
2 teaspoons cinnamon
   powder
1 teaspoon ground
   coriander
1 large carrot, grated
40g raisins or sultanas
30g desiccated
   coconut
40g seed mix

**Vanilla Butter Icing:**
50g butter
100g cream cheese
200–275g icing sugar
1 teaspoon vanilla
   essence or paste

I put this recipe together one day to try to get my family away from their chocolate muffin addiction. They are lovely – especially warm with a little plain yoghurt for an alternative breakfast treat. I use a seed mix, which contains omega rich flax, sunflower, poppy and pumpkin seeds, but feel free to experiment with your own versions.

- Preheat the halogen oven using the preheat setting or set the temperature to 200°C.
- Cream the butter and sugar together until pale and fluffy. Add the eggs a little at a time and continue to beat well. Sift the flour and fold into the mixture gently.
- When thoroughly mixed, add the cinnamon, coriander, carrot, raisins, coconut and seeds and combine well.
- Place the mixture in cupcake or muffin cases in a muffin or cupcake tray. I have not been able to find a round muffin tray, so I use silicon muffin cases and place them on the halogen baking trays that come with the accessory packs. You can comfortably fit 10 on the tray. This recipe should make 8–12 cakes depending on their size.
- Place on the low rack and cook for 15–18 minutes. The cakes should be firm and spring back when touched. Place on a cooling rack to cool.

- While the cakes are cooling, prepare the icing. Beat the butter and cream cheese together until soft. Gradually add the icing sugar and vanilla essence and beat until you reach the desired consistency – it should be glossy, thick and lump free. The best way of testing to see if you have added enough icing sugar is to taste it. It should taste sweet and creamy but not too buttery.
- If you are using silicon muffin cases, wait until the cakes are cool, then carefully pull away at the sides of each case. Once the case is clear all the way around, turn it upside down and the cake should pop out.
- Place the icing into an icing bag and fold down the ends to secure. Start in the centre of each cooled cake and spiral outwards covering the whole of the cake top, gently overlapping to avoid gaps. Finish with a sprinkle of cinnamon powder and you are ready to serve.

SUITABLE FOR VEGETARIANS

# Meal Planners

Meal planners have been very popular in my previous books so we have included them in this cookbook also. Meal planners are designed to make your life easier and to save you money. Until you plan your meals, you will not appreciate how much money you can save on your weekly food shopping. It is estimated that over a third of our food shopping is wasted every week. If you plan your meals, you tend to buy only what you need and therefore avoid waste and unnecessary purchases.

Here is a selection of meal plans for your main meals only and shopping lists to help get you started. I have included four weeks for those who eat meat and fish, and two weeks for vegetarians. The recipes included in this book appear in the meal planners in italics.

# Meat and fish meal planners

## WEEK 1

**Shopping list**

1 whole chicken

1 red onion

1 lemon

3–4kg potatoes

Seasonal veg for 4 meals

Salad for 2 meals

3 onions

1 pack of celery

75g button mushrooms

100g ham

1 can condensed chicken or mushroom
  soup

1 pack of puff pastry

1 pack of filo pastry

500g fish fillets

200g salmon

400g haddock fillets

100g prawns

75g cheese

125g gruyère cheese

50g parmesan cheese

800g minced beef

1 chilli

5 eggs

300g spaghetti

1 tin tomatoes

1 bulb of garlic

400g baby leaf spinach

**Store cupboard essentials**

| | | |
|---|---|---|
| Olive oil | Cumin | Basil |
| Tarragon | Chilli powder | Nutmeg |
| Paprika | Worcestershire sauce | Sesame seeds |
| Milk | Parsley | Coriander |
| Butter | Breadcrumbs | Tomato purée |
| Flour | Sugar | Oats |
| Mustard | Salt and pepper | Gravy |

# Meals • WEEK 1

**Sunday:** *Roast Chicken*, roast potatoes, two seasonal vegetables and gravy
* Buy a chicken that is slightly bigger than your needs, but make sure it fits in your halogen oven! You will then be able to strip it of meat (thighs, legs, breast and even turn the bird over to pull off the meat). Put the leftover meat to one side ready for baking a chicken pie for tomorrow's dinner – plus, if you have any extra, you can use it to make sandwiches.
* When cooking the chicken, make room in the halogen for your roast potatoes.

**Monday:** *Cheat's Leftover Chicken Pie*, two vegetables and mash
* Prepare double the mash and keep it in the fridge for tomorrow's fish pie.

**Tuesday:** *Creamy Fish Pie* and vegetables
* You already have the mash prepared from yesterday's meal, so now all you have to do is prepare the fish pie.

**Wednesday:** *Spicy Meatballs in Rich Tomato Sauce*
* This can be prepared in advance, or why not double up the recipe and freeze the second portion for another meal?
* Serve with spaghetti.

**Thursday:** *Spinach and Feta Pie* served with new potatoes and salad or vegetables
* This is a really light pie, so serve it with salad or fresh vegetables.

**Friday:** *Beef Burgers*, *Potato Wedges* and salad
* Remember you can double up this recipe and freeze until needed.
* Place the potato wedges in the oven and, when you are ready to cook the burgers, you can leave the wedges on the low rack and grill the burgers on the top rack.

**Saturday:** *Haddock, Egg and Gruyère Bake*
* Serve with green vegetables.

# Meat and fish meal planners

WEEK 2

**Shopping list**

Beef joint

2kg potatoes

2kg new potatoes

Seasonal vegetables for 4 meals

Seasonal salad for 2 meals

4 fish fillets

1 large bulb of fennel

1 bulb of garlic

2 onions

4 lemons

200g mushrooms

300g button mushrooms

300ml sour cream

300g spaghetti or tagliatelle

Fresh herbs (e.g. parsley and dill)

4 salmon fillets

50g parmesan cheese

2 leeks

1 bunch of spring onions

300g chicken pieces

4 chicken breasts

300ml chicken stock

6 slices Parma ham

100g French beans

300g crème fraîche

50g watercress

150g prawns

500g salmon

50g baby leaf spinach

½ pack of puff pastry

1 tub of cream cheese

1 large tomato

**Store cupboard essentials**

Dark brown sugar

Maple or golden syrup

Horseradish

Butter

Olive oil

Tarragon

Dried onion

Dried chives

Red wine

White wine

Cornflour

Paprika

Milk

Mustard

Sesame seeds

Cayenne pepper

Tabasco sauce

Salt and pepper

Mixed herbs

# Meals • WEEK 2

**Sunday:** *Roast Beef and Horseradish,* roast potatoes and two vegetables
- Buy a beef joint that is slightly bigger than your needs but make sure it fits in your halogen oven! Put the leftover meat to one side ready for Tuesday's stroganoff – plus, if you have any extra, you can use it to make sandwiches.
- When cooking the beef, make room in the halogen for your roast potatoes.

**Monday:** *One Pot Roasted Fish, Fennel and Red Onion*
- You could serve this with additional vegetables or potatoes if you wish.

**Tuesday:** *Beef Stroganoff*
- Serve with tagliatelle or spaghetti.

**Wednesday:** *Salmon and Herb Butter Parcels*
- Serve with new potatoes or *Cheese Crunch New Potatoes* and green vegetables.

**Thursday:** *Chicken and Mushroom Casserole*
- You could serve this with *Baked New Potatoes.*

**Friday:** *Salmon and Prawn Puff Pie*
- Serve with salad or green vegetables.

**Saturday:** *Hot Stuffed Chicken with Parma Ham*
- Serve with *Fan Potatoes* and two veg.

# Meat and fish meal planners

WEEK 3

**Shopping list**

Lamb joint

4kg potatoes

2 sweet potatoes

Seasonal vegetables for 3 meals

Seasonal salad ingredients for 3 meals

1 bulb of garlic

2 chillies

5 eggs

1 bunch of spring onions

2 red peppers

6 rashers of pancetta

1 jar of sundried tomatoes in oil

125g parmesan cheese

3 red onions

1 onion

800g haddock fillets

1 lemon

150ml crème fraîche

500g bread flour

1 sachet of dried yeast

Chosen pizza toppings

4 carrots

400g lamb mince

75g mushrooms

150g mature cheddar

1 knuckle fresh ginger

1 lime

4 lime leaves

2 sticks of lemongrass

Thai paste

1 tin of coconut milk

150ml Greek yoghurt

4 fish fillets

400g Thai Lime Rice

175g macaroni

8 rashers of bacon

3 leeks

| Store cupboard essentials | Butter | Worcestershire sauce |
|---|---|---|
| Rosemary (dried and fresh) | Milk | Semolina |
| Fresh basil, oregano or thyme | Brown sugar | Cornflour |
| Fresh coriander | Olive oil | Mustard |
| Mixed dried herbs | Paprika | Breadcrumbs |
| Parsley | Yeast extract | Oats |
| | Red wine | Salt and pepper |
| | Gravy | |

# Meals • WEEK 3

**Sunday:** *Roast Leg of Lamb with Roasted Vegetables*
- When cooking the lamb, make room in the halogen for your roast vegetables.

**Monday:** *Mediterranean-style Tortilla*
- Serve with a lovely salad.

**Tuesday:** *Creamy Baked Haddock*
- Serve with *Fan Potatoes* and vegetables.

**Wednesday:** *Homemade Pizza*
- You can double up the dough recipe and place the pizza bases in the freezer until needed.
- Choose your own toppings.
- Serve with *Potato Wedges* and salad.

**Thursday:** *Shepherd's Pie*
- A one-pot family favourite – serve it with vegetables and homemade gravy.
- Again, you could double up the recipe and freeze one pie for another meal.

**Friday:** *Thai Fish Bakes*
- Serve with steamed new potatoes or on a bed of rice and with your choice of vegetables.

**Saturday:** Bacon, Leek and Macaroni Cheese Bake
- A filling and satisfying one-pot meal.

# Meat and fish meal planners

WEEK 4

**Shopping list**

1 whole chicken

3kg potatoes

2 lemons

Seasonal veg for 3 meals

Seasonal salad for 3 meals

2 aubergines

5 red onions

1 bulb of garlic

4 peppers

400g lean mince

75g mushrooms

150g button mushrooms

4 tomatoes

50g mature cheddar

4 mackerels

400ml crème fraîche

75g gruyère cheese

4 chicken breasts

1 pack of pancetta

2 tins of chopped tomatoes

1kg new potatoes

400g tinned tuna

200g sweetcorn (tinned or frozen)

1 bunch of spring onions

Lasagne sheets

500ml passata

50g parmesan

8 lean sausages

6 rashers of bacon or lardons

1 sweet potato

1 punnet of cherry tomatoes

1 ball of mozzarella or 110g goats'
cheese

500g bread flour

1 sachet of yeast

**Store cupboard essentials**

| | | |
|---|---|---|
| Paprika | Mixed herbs | Fresh basil |
| Olive oil | Milk | Fresh parsley |
| Butter | Nutmeg | Salt and pepper |
| Red wine | Sundried tomato purée | Sugar |
| Tarragon | Stock | Balsamic vinegar |

# Meals • WEEK 4

**Sunday:** *Roast Chicken*, roast potatoes and two veg
- Buy a chicken that is slightly bigger than your needs. If you have some left over, you can use it to make sandwiches.
- When cooking the chicken, make room for your roast potatoes.

**Monday:** *Stuffed Aubergine Bolognaise*
- Double up the bolognaise recipe so that you have it ready for a spaghetti bolognaise, lasagne, chilli con carne or as a topping for jacket potatoes.

**Tuesday:** *Simple Mackerel Parcels*
- Serve with *Cheesy Dauphine Potatoes* and vegetables.

**Wednesday:** *Chicken Italiano*
- Serve with *Baked New Potatoes* and fresh seasonal vegetables.

**Thursday:** *Tuna and Sweetcorn Lasagne*
- Double up the recipe and freeze one lasagne for another meal. Remember to label and date any frozen meals.
- Serve with *Potato Wedges* and salad.

**Friday:** *Sausage Casserole*
- Serve with mash potato.

**Saturday:** *Upside Down Pizza Bake*
- Serve with a selection of salads.

# Vegetarian meal planners

WEEK 1

**Shopping list**

| | |
|---|---|
| 1–2 butternut squash | 4 aubergines |
| 120g mushrooms | 3 red peppers |
| 75g cashew nuts | 1 courgette |
| 330g goats' cheese | 2–3 carrots |
| 3kg potatoes | 1 bulb of celery |
| 5 red onions | 8 ripe tomatoes |
| 1 bulb of garlic | 1 tin chopped tomatoes |
| Seasonal veg for 3 meals | 50g parmesan |
| Seasonal salad for 3 meals | 150g mature cheddar |
| Filo pastry | 5 eggs |
| 370g feta cheese | 1 bunch of spring onions |
| 450g baby leaf spinach | 1 jar sundried tomatoes in oil |
| 2kg new potatoes | 1 tin of tomatoes |
| 500g bread flour | 1kg sweet potatoes |
| 1 sachet of yeast | 400g veggie mince |
| Chosen pizza toppings | 300ml crème fraîche |

**Store cupboard essentials**

| | | |
|---|---|---|
| Butter | Fresh thyme | Oats |
| Olive oil | Fresh bay leaves | Dried mint |
| Paprika | Mixed fresh herbs | Ground cinnamon |
| Salt and pepper | Sugar | Vegetable stock |
| Mixed herbs | Balsamic vinegar | Tomato purée |
| Nutmeg | Red wine | Plain flour |
| Sesame seeds | Breadcrumbs | |

# Meals • WEEK 1

**Sunday:** *Butternut Squash Stuffed with Mushroom, Cashew Nut and Goat's Cheese*
• Serve with *Fan Potatoes* and seasonal vegetables.

**Monday:** *Spinach and Feta Pie*
• Serve with new potatoes and green vegetables.

**Tuesday:** *Homemade Pizza*
• Serve with *Potato Wedges* and salad.

**Wednesday:** *Ratatouille and Feta Gratin*
• Serve with crusty bread and salad.

**Thursday:** *Sundried Tomato and Goat's Cheese Frittata*
• Serve with a variety of salads.

**Friday:** *Vegetable Crumble*
• Serve with sweet potato mash and seasonal vegetables.

**Saturday:** *Vegetarian Moussaka*
• Double up the bolognaise mixture as it can be frozen and used for spaghetti bolognaise, lasagne or even as a topping for jacket potatoes.

# Vegetarian meal planners

## WEEK 2

### Shopping list

| | |
|---|---|
| 2kg potatoes | 1 cauliflower |
| 2kg sweet potatoes | 50g cashew nuts |
| 2kg new potatoes | 100ml natural yoghurt |
| 8 carrots | 150g parmesan cheese |
| 4 leeks | Lasagne sheets |
| 2 heads of broccoli | 100g mushrooms |
| 600g baby leaf spinach | 1 tub of ricotta |
| 16 tomatoes | 5 red peppers |
| 350g mature cheddar | 12–15 cherry tomatoes |
| Seasonal veg for 4 meals | 1 tin chopped tomatoes |
| 1 tin chickpeas | 1 jar pasta sauce |
| 1 pack of tofu | 1 small pumpkin or squash |
| 5 onions | 1 lemon |
| 1 chilli | Knuckle of root ginger |
| Celery | Crusty bread |
| 6–8 wholemeal baps | Hummus |
| Salad for 3 meals | |

### Store cupboard essentials

| | | |
|---|---|---|
| Butter | Tomato purée | Balsamic vinegar |
| Plain flour | Garam masala | Sugar |
| Milk | Soy sauce | Vegetable stock |
| Mustard | Breadcrumbs | Mixed fresh herbs |
| Nutmeg | Oats | Ground coriander |
| Sesame seeds | Self-raising flour | Salt and pepper |
| Olive oil | Fresh thyme | |

# Meals • WEEK 2

**Sunday:** *Eco-Warrior Pie*
- This can be a one-pot dish or you can add some extra vegetables to accompany it.

**Monday:** *Tofu and Chickpea Burgers*
- Serve with *Potato Wedges* or chips and salad.
- You can double up this recipe and freeze the extra burgers ready for another meal.

**Tuesday:** *Vegetable Cheesy Cobbler*
- This can be a one-pot meal – just add some extra seasonal veg or a green salad to accompany it.

**Wednesday:** *Spinach and Ricotta Lasagne*
- Serve with a selection of salads.

**Thursday:** *Roasted Tomato and Garlic Peppers*
- Serve with *Cheese Crunch New Potatoes*.

**Friday:** *Vegetable Crumble*
- Double up the recipe and make one for the freezer, ready for another meal.

**Saturday:** *Roasted Pumpkin Soup*
- Double up the recipe and store the extra soup in the fridge or freezer, ready for a snack or another meal.
- Serve with crusty bread and homemade hummus.

# Index